Takir the Weight

Life from Apprentice to Tool Van Supervisor
at Thornaby Traction Maintenance Depot

1962 to 1990

Bob Willis

ISBN No. 978-0-9928999-0-5

First published April 2014

Printed by Burgess Design and Print.
Beehive Street, Retford, Nottinghamshire DN22 6JE
www.burgessdesignandprint.com

Contents

TAKING THE WEIGHT

Foreword

Have you ever said to yourself "I could write a book about that . . . "

I heard Bob Willis say it on several occasions, over a number of years, too many to mention. He has finally got around to it, and what follows is a glimpse into his railway career, following a path that had its up and downs, (no pun intended, but it fits as you will see) gaining an insight into what it was like to be a young engineer finding his feet in a rapidly changing industry – the end of the steam era and the coming of the diesel age.

His story begins when he leaves school with a determination to become a railwayman, follows him through his apprenticeship years and then on to his grown up days as a diesel fitter. He then moves on to the subject that became the mainstay of his career – derailments, or more specifically re-railing and recovery, and he tells us what it's like to work in a motive power depot and of the various tasks he was involved with.

Along the way, Bob tells of the characters he worked with and the experiences he went through. I can concur to a lot of these tales because, like Bob, I was an apprentice at Thornaby, but 7 years his junior, starting work in 1969. Unlike him, I was to become an electrician and our paths didn't cross for almost 10 years, but in the subsequent years up to his retirement in 2007, we often worked together on numerous technical issues. As our careers progressed through various technical and managerial roles, we became close friends and survived the wave of "new" rail freight companies brought about by privatisation, both of us managing to remain based at Thornaby.

In the late 1990s, I was appointed as Technical Engineer, bringing with it an on-call responsibility. This meant I was one of three local engineers whose role was to deal with serious incidents in the North East region, including derailments.

Up until then, I had managed to avoid anything to do with re-railing – the 76 tonne crane was a total mystery, and jacks and packing a dark art indeed - but as I was expected to be able to take on the role of Recovery Engineer in overall charge of the engineering staff on site, I had to learn. There followed lots of formal training to get the certificate to say I was competent, but the real training came from the Breakdown Supervisors, and I very quickly learned that they were the men to listen to. Bob Willis was one of these men, very experienced, very capable, very respected by his men – although I was to find that he and other recovery supervisors like him weren't too keen on having us managers on the job.

As you read Bob's fascinating accounts of the incidents he was involved with in the 70s and 80s, it is apparent that, whilst he had an immense amount of responsibility, he also had the freedom to get on with the job. Underlying this, he reveals himself to be an accomplished engineer, a man with an eye for detail and a talent for getting things right.

All in all, not too bad for a trainspotter . . .

Brian Cheetham

Regional Technical Engineer (retd)
Thornaby
3 July 2007

Acknowledgements

This book wouldn't have appeared without my Team at Thornaby. One night shift tea break in 2005 in my office, we were talking about the 'Good Old Days' and as I talked about my Tool van years they came up with the thought that I should put my experiences into print so they didn't get lost. So thank you Frankie Cox, Geoff Tew, Colin Austin, Tony Wyldbore, Willie Winter, Mick Payne, Derek Slack, Stephen Bainbridge, Peter Gordge, and Malcolm Ripley.

The help I had obtaining information and photographs is all down to Dick Watson, Brian Cheetham, Maurice Burns, Phil Thickett and John Cook. A big thank you to Burgess Design and Print for advice and making sense of everything I threw at them to finally produce this book.

Once roughly written down or typed out, our friend, Pauline, used her expertise in proof reading, grammar and layout.

Thanks must go to my wife Dot and my family, for firstly putting up with me disappearing from home at all the inconvenient times of the day and night when the kids were young, sometimes for long periods. Secondly for putting up with me when spending hours bashing away at the keyboard, (even when visiting our son in California) scribbling away on a writing pad on holiday in Majorca, or being hidden away for hours on end in my room peering at the computer screen while I wished things made more sense.

Finally, a big thank you, and a dedication, to everyone at Thornaby TMD and wherever the Tool vans worked. Also, to those who I worked with, in whatever capacity, for making what could be a tough job at times, very interesting.

I apologise if I have missed someone's name or got their name wrong - one of my major failings throughout life has been my inability to remember names!

Photographs are as credited, and any that are not credited are mine. Any errors please let me know so I can correct this. All photographs remain the property of the copyright holders.

R. Willis

About me

My life away from the railway

I am married to Dot and have two sons, Matthew and Jamie. Probably having got fed up with my singing and model engineering hobby some years ago, the eldest son, Matthew, decided to get away as far as he could to live, and he is now married with two children and working in San Jose, California. Jamie only managed to get as far as Manchester, and is now married and working over there. (Over there, as it's not in Yorkshire...) Dot didn't manage to get away at all!

Whilst railway work was a large part of my life, believe it or not I do have other interests. Whilst at school, singing was a talent I had nurtured by the music teacher at Marton Grove School. I joined the local church choir, and I haven't stopped singing in church choirs since. Having started at St Chad's Church, eventually, some years later that choir faded away, and after a time I found out that a new apprentice at Thornaby (thanks John A), sang in the choir at St Paul's Church, Thornaby, led by Alan Barber, so I joined that, but again, the choir ceased, due to the Alan retiring. Eventually, in 1984 I joined the choir under Geoff Hill at St Mary's Church, Acklam, Middlebrough, and have been there ever since. Being at St Mary's has meant my getting involved in church activities, and ending up on various committees.

Whilst at St Paul's I was asked to join a singing group called 'Pieces of Eight', directed by Alan Barber's brother, George, who was Choirmaster at St Peter's Church, Stockton. This 'acapella' (unaccompanied singing) group gives concerts of secular music wherever asked, but usually in churches or church halls to raise funds, though we have sung in the Empire Theatre at Sunderland, The Rowntree Theatre in York, and other large venues, even being a 'time filler' before Rowan Atkinson did his act at the Stockton Empire. Another "Pieces of Eight" success was winning, several years in succession, the competition for best singing act on Radio Tees. The group even appeared on Cilla Black's TV show 'Surprise, Surprise'!!

Being sort of linked to St Peter's by "Pieces of Eight" I have been a part time member of that choir for a number of years, and this has enabled me to take part in several choir trips abroad, singing in the great churches and cathedrals in France, Germany, Belgium and Holland.

At Metz Cathedral, Lorraine, France, 2003

TAKING THE WEIGHT

My 55xx tank running at Brent Hudsons track, Swavesy, near Cambridge

My other hobby has been model engineering. Having gone along to the Middlesbrough Model Engineering track in Albert Park, Middlesbrough, when I was 14 years old, this sparked something, which I still enjoy. I eventually became Chairman for a couple of years before leaving. I completed my own 5" gauge loco in 1984 and in the same year became a member of the Ryedale Society of Model Engineers at Gilling East, which was just establishing itself, and building a ground level track. Again, after a few years I became Chairman there, and have been (apart from two years), for more years than I can remember.

The RSME has always aimed to run to a full size railway ethos, so there are signal boxes, and a fully signalled double track main line etc.

As we wanted to play trains this meant wagons were needed, so I have built ten wagons now, and there are probably more to come. There is something about taking pieces of plain metal and turning them into a scale working replica of the full size.

All in all, I don't have a lot of time to sit around twiddling my thumbs!!

My model of a BR trestle wagon (I built two, mad!).

TAKING THE WEIGHT

Life at Thornaby Depot 1962 – 1990 and Tool Van days

Apprenticeship

L eaving school in early August 1962 I determined, as all sensible boys do, that I wanted to be an engine driver and duly sent off a letter to the North Eastern Region of British Railways to that effect. Having somehow managed to get onto a school trip to Paris (even though I had left school by then) I got back home to find a letter waiting, inviting me for an interview with the Area Engineer, Mr Clothier and his assistant Mr Jefferson on a date whilst I was away. As we didn't have a phone my mother had got the bus and gone to Zetland house, seen Mr Clothier's secretary and negotiated another date after I had arrived back - thanks mum. This took place in Zetland House which was a newly erected, typical 1960's monstrosity (thankfully since demolished) attached to Middlesbrough station.

When I arrived at Zetland house it was a bit disconcerting to find I was the last of 35 boys for interview (but better than the hundreds that now chase after one job). The opening part of the interview began "Now Mr Willis I understand you want to become an engine driver??" "Yes sir" "Well we haven't any vacancies for engine cleaners (the first rung on the ladder to becoming a driver) at the moment, but looking at your school reports and results we consider you are too clever to be an engine driver, so would you consider becoming a diesel fitter??" (Now those more discerning amongst you reading this will realise what those few words actually meant!) Little time was given to my being able to digest what was being said as they wanted an answer there and then, so 'yes' was the reply, little knowing where that would lead in the years to come. Then followed some basic questions, remembering that I had just left a secondary modern school where the only engineering taught was woodwork!! Questions such as; explain a four stroke cycle and a two stroke cycle; how does a bicycle freewheel work? Why do engines need oil in them? and more in that vein, came as a shock. I think having started going to the Middlesbrough Model Engineering Society track in Albert Park a few years earlier helped a bit. But somehow I must have impressed them as at the end, after sending me out of the room I was called back in after what seemed an eternity, and told I would be given a five year apprenticeship as a diesel fitter, details would be in the post. I had to go for a medical and if successful come back with my parents to sign all the forms.

After the obligatory visit to the railway doctor (based in small grubby premises next to the main locomotive works at the corner of Denmark street and the old A1 road at Darlington) for various tests including of course "please cough", and try to distinguish colours from a well fingered dirty set of coloured silk threads, I then sat at home waiting for the final letter. This eventually arrived saying to go back to Zetland House with a parent to sign up. Mr Clothier was waiting and before signing he explained that they were taking two apprentices on that year and I had been chosen to take part in an experiment, in that I would go straight onto a full time, one year course at Darlington Technical College. The other apprentice would start straight away at Thornaby Depot and just do one day and one night a week at college as previous apprentices had. This of course meant I was at a disadvantage as I didn't actually set foot into Thornaby depot until the week before Christmas, whereas Tony Young had already been there three and a half months. But officially my railway career had started on the 17th September 1962. After I finished college in 1963 it was decided that all new apprentices would attend college for their first year and this continued until the system changed completely in the seventies.

College

Having just left school, full time college wasn't what I had had in mind when starting on the railway, and as all the other students worked for Cleveland Bridge, Darlington Forge or Whessoe (large engineering firms) in Darlington and were training to be machinists or erecting fitters and not diesel fitters, the course was tailored to machining and general maths etc to suit their needs. It stood me in good stead of course when I later took up model engineering. I must have been bored, as very little of that year has stayed with me; though I can remember that one day towards the end of our year there we were allowed to have a go on the college Go-Cart on the college field. One of our class was a rather tall gangly youth and somehow he got his foot jammed in the pedals which resulted in the Go-Cart going round like a scalded cat until he eventually lost control of the steering and plunged through the perimeter fence into a rather posh garden, demolishing a cold frame and badly damaging a greenhouse before it finally stopped in a cabbage patch with him still in the seat. Another not so pleasant memory was the class bully who deliberately turned a lathe on as someone was changing the speed via a vee belt, trapping his fingers badly. Strangely the victim was his pal (!) who followed the bully around like a lapdog and still continued to do so afterwards.

First time at the depot

My first appearance at the depot was therefore a highlight for me, a brand new world, procedures to learn, arriving at 07.30 and getting one's time book with my pay number '1081', finding an empty locker to take over, getting and fixing a lock to it, were all new experiences for a mere bairn, lots of new faces to put names to and more importantly remember!! (I've never been good at remembering names). The working week was Monday-Friday 7.30am to 4.30pm and 7am to 2pm on a Saturday.

Tommy Brownless's office to right. Camera is between 5 and 6 roads.
The wheel lathe would eventually be placed immediately left on 6 road.   BR

In the workshop Tommy Brownless was the key figure, wearing a brown smock, whereas Mr Wrightson was the Maintenance Supervisor with an office in the main office block, he was always smartly dressed in a dark suit and of course a trilby hat. Tom was only the charge hand, but everything hinged around him. At 7.05am everyone was stood outside his little office in the main shed, he would come out with a handful of repair cards and swiftly go round giving them to the staff with a brief explanation of what was required if that was needed, which, on my first day left me stood there alone. Tommy stared and said "Who the hell are you?" An explanation jogged his memory and he shouted for Tony Young to come over and show me round the depot and explain what was what and more importantly meet all the other apprentices of which there were at least twenty; this took all day. Until that point, Tony didn't even know that I even existed and was a bit miffed that he wasn't at full time college, but we got on well for the remainder of the five years. The following day I was again left until the last by Tommy and he just said you're with Jack Lack, who I didn't know from

TAKING THE WEIGHT

Adam!! Eventually I found Jack with his mate Colin Brookes standing looking at 76024, a standard 2-6-0 class 4 which was outside 7 road in steam. After a brief introduction, next thing I'm up on top of the boiler with a few big spanners and more importantly a big hammer, dealing with a sticking clack valve while Jack shouted instructions from below. The similarity between the job I was doing and Jack's name suddenly clicked with me, and I never did pick up the courage to ask if it was his real name, though of course, like all Jacks, he was actually christened John.

I should explain that in late 1962 80% of the loco's at Thornaby were still steam loco's, there only being a handful of Sulzer type 2s allocated. These were looked after by a couple of fitters who had been selected and been on courses, and the oldest apprentices were put with them to get experience before coming out of their time. I can remember that we had Q6s, J27s, lots of WD 2-8-0's a few V2s for fast freights, J72 and J94 tank locos for yard shunting, also a few V3 tanks and a couple of standard 2-6-0s. As soon as a batch of diesels appeared though, a larger number of steam loco's would be sent off to Darlington or West Hartlepool to finish their working lives, or at worst sent for scrap.

J26 65755 and a WD 2-8-0 on repair in 7 road. Note Tool vans on left on 9 road.   BR

The other people in charge were the shed master, Jack (John) Wandless and the maintenance Supervisor. He had a shop office man (clerk) an ex fitter's labourer who had to be on light duties, Jack (John) Clare, who knew where every bit of paper was about every engine and how the whole complicated paper process worked. There were chargehand boilersmiths and chargehand labourers, but at that time they passed me by and we didn't meet. The office staff upstairs comprised of a chief clerk and a lot of female clerks, who to us down on the floor were like a god with his angels, spoken of in hushed tones and never to be spoken to, as they were in a different world to the shop floor. The only time we came into contact with them was on Thursday – pay day, when two would be in the pay office to exchange your brass token (with your pay number on it) for a pay packet. Or if you thought your pay was wrong you went upstairs to a little lift up window, knocked carefully and stood waiting for one of the staff to come and answer your query.

B1 61304 in the roundhouse where boiler washouts and repairs were carried out no matter what the weather was like. Maurice Burns

TAKING THE WEIGHT

Back to Jack Lack. Being nearly 65 his role on the depot was doing the small jobs, in effect light duties, so clacks, safety valves, gauge glasses, injector and vacuum ejector faults all came his way. I soon realised that despite being ordinary workmen he and Colin were gentlemen. Not a swear word passed their lips and they had a large breadth of knowledge, being able to talk about anything.

Once Christmas was over (only Christmas Day and New Year's Day off!) the weather hit hard and I can remember struggling to work on my push bike trying to follow bus tracks with at least six inches of snow on the roads, then getting docked for being ten minutes late. I spent a whole week in the round shed; there was water everywhere as the boilersmiths were washing out loco's and I followed up doing gauge glass renewals along with the shut off cock packing being renewed and the waterways in the fittings being rodded through. I don't know what the temperature was but the only heating was an occasional large coal brazier between roads which had no effect on the temperature in a freezing cold steam engine cab. Losing the feeling in one's fingers was a continual hazard, so recourse to a brazier was often. I can recall a particular J94 that took six new gauge glasses before I got one to stay in one piece, as one by one they cracked as I tightened up the gland nuts. I mentioned to the fire raiser to keep an eye on it when he got up steam but he just laughed and said "Oh didn't Jack warn you about that one?" "It'll be alright once it gets warm". Of course, Jack hadn't mentioned it; he wanted me to learn the hard way and to figure out that the fittings were out of line slightly on the backhead ever since it had come out of Darlington works.

The shed shunting was done by a dedicated crew using a J72 0-6-0 tank loco which, whilst of a North Eastern Railway design of 1898, was actually built at Darlington Works in 1950! It was usually 69005 though others were available. The loco and crew were referred to for some reason as the 'shed cat' and that name stuck right up to the end of a dedicated shunting team. The shunter was a tall chap, an ex main line guard who was approaching retirement. He was of the old school and a gentle person who would do any shunting around the shed that anybody wanted, without any fuss.

V2 60808 stands outside the straight shed   John Cook

One day it had been snowing hard all night and was still snowing during the day. I was working at the west end of the shed when there was a dull thump and as I headed to where the noise had come from a fitter stopped me and said "Don't go down there son".

What had happened was the shunter had gone to open the big wooden doors on the end of three road and the door had come off its hinges and down on top of the unfortunate chap. The blacksmith, whose shop was right next to the door, had rushed out and single handed lifted the corner of the door whilst someone else dragged the crushed shunter out from underneath. He was rushed to hospital with severe injuries from which he never really recovered.

The cause of the door coming down was quite basic; the doors which had two per opening were made of wood, very large and heavy (see photo) and had two huge hinges that each had a ball on the end. Set into the concrete door frames were corresponding cast iron cups that the ball ends sat in. As the snow was deep, when the door was opened the snow formed a wedge that lifted the door so that the ball end came out of the cup causing the door to fall down. I would hate to think how much those doors weighed. A few days later the door was repaired and lifted back into place with a P'way crane then every door had a piece of angle bolted above the cup to stop it lifting.

The door on the right was the one that fell down on the unfortunate shunter.
V3 67620 on 5 road and Q6 63437 on 4 road stand outside.   Maurice Burns

The Easter break from college put me with Jack again, but by then there were more diesels and less steam loco's and Jack had been trained to overhaul diesel injectors. So I spent most of my time cleaning injector nozzles, lapping in needles and finally testing them. Everything was spotlessly clean with racks of used dirty and clean injectors at separate ends of the room. The routine was occasionally broken by going to work on steam loco's but the writing was on the wall. One of the older apprentices, John Cook, took me onto an English Electric type 4 that was sat outside on full revs, all the top hats (cylinder covers) were off and I was stood nose up against a whirl of tappets and push rods and an unbelievable noise, (no ear protection then).

In those first months on the depot there was lots to take in, and seeing Archie Dent, a little wiry fitter, removing side rods and lowering wheels out of a Q6 0-8-0 on the drops was an education in what could be achieved quickly with a hammer and chisel and a ¼ hammer. Dave Ruddick was another who did the same, whilst chewing away on the stem of his pipe which never left his mouth. Smoke box jobs on main steam pipes and superheaters weren't liked for obvious reasons and I can remember a WD 2-8-0 sitting at the end of 5 road for ages whilst a struggle to remove the piston valves for a ring check and carbon removal took place. Then there was Ralph Easby one of the fitters who had been chosen to be trained up on the new-fangled diesels and he was becoming expert at dealing with all aspects of these loco's from removing pistons and liners to exhauster or compressor removal and overhauls. In those days running depots would repair small components like compressors etc. rather than get an overhauled unit from the works.

There was a turner, 'Tashy' Ayres who worked wonders on a centre lathe and shaping machine, he did anything and everything on them, from machining pins for brake gear, to pipework flanges. There was also a vertical boring machine for machining axle boxes, and last but not least a huge lathe for re-profiling steam loco wheelsets and axle journals. 'Tashy' did this just using callipers and a rule, none of the modern gadgets then, especially at a running shed, though he did have a small micrometer that came out of its immaculate box when doing something really technical.

Two coppersmiths were employed, Lenny Sherris and Arthur (surname forgotten). They could lay their hands to anything in that line, making or repairing pipework with complicated bends in any size, making oil bottles or tins for the stores shelves and lots more. Lenny was the one who re-metalled with white metal, axle boxes that had run hot. When the steam loco's started to slowly disappear, Arthur retired, but Lenny was still needed to repair pipework etc. and had also now learnt how to repair windscreen wiper motors and washers along with route indicators.

Tashy, Lenny and Arthur were true craftsmen and the skills they employed in their crafts were a pleasure to watch.

Full time at the depot

In the July I took my exams at Darlington Technical College with favourable results and went to Thornaby full time at last. Being the youngest apprentice I was given some strange duties. Having been deemed to be competent on diesel injectors, I was often sent with an ex driver Harry Mudd, whose sole task was to get a list of UVS's (Urgent Vehicle Standing forms) from the stores office and then walk up the track side to Thornaby Station and go by train to Darlington North Road station, walk to the main works, present the UVS's to a clerk there and wait for a few hours before collecting the various parts from the works stores, putting them in a large poacher's bag he had, and returning to Thornaby. I soon realised that when I went it was because there was something large or heavy to collect, it not being unknown for me to stagger back with a bottom body side panel for a Sulzer 2, as they were the first bits of bodywork to suffer damage in the occasional side swipes that happened with wagons in the many yards of that time. After a few months, whenever Harry was off I was sent on my own. At least these trips gave me the chance to wander around the works collecting loco numbers, seeing how things were done to steam loco's that were still being repaired there. I went often until the works shut in 1965 and in all that time wandering around on my own no one ever asked me who I was or why I was there.

Loose roof

While the steam engines were still at Thornaby the shed layout was such that they came onto the shed, were coaled and watered then came onto the ashpit roads for the fire to be cleaned or dropped, depending on where they were going next. Part of this process was for the loco to be examined by an examining fitter for defects and to check any repairs a driver may have booked, Charlie Church and Vince Brennan being names that spring to mind doing that job.

They had a little cabin that was on the side of the ash pit shed where they made their paperwork out and of course there just happened by chance to be some comfy chairs and benches in there, as well as a compulsory guards' stove with a chimney that went through the corrugated iron roof. Jack Forster (Black Jack) as well as being a good fitter, was one of those mischievous types and he knew their sleep patterns, sorry, work patterns, and late one winter's afternoon he crept over and onto the roof. The apprentices knew what was afoot and all stood to watch from the safety of the repair shed doors. Jack stood next to the chimney and calmly dropped two detonators down it and then jumped off and ran away as fast as he could to hide. Nothing happened for a few minutes and then there was an almighty bang, a jet black stream of soot and smoke shot out of the chimney, at the same time as the roof leapt up and the door to the cabin flew open with a stream of smoke and soot shooting out, followed by four unrecognizable soot covered bodies. The language was quite unprintable as they tried to find out who had done it and where he was, but Jack had covered his tracks well and they never found out, and we weren't saying. Needless to say, it took a few days to get the cabin back into a liveable condition.

Private loco's.

I then spent six months with fitter Jack (John) Neville, who had the onerous task of examining all the private loco's that the steelworks and other firms owned, and had been given official written permission to run over BR lines and sidings on the condition they were examined by BR staff once a year. In the early sixties there were at least a hundred in the area covered by Thornaby; mainly they were in the several steel works that bordered both sides of the Middlesbrough to Redcar line for several miles. But there were oddities such as two immaculate fireless loco's up on the top of the cliffs above Saltburn at Skinningrove Steel Works and a beautifully kept, very small, 0-4-0 tank loco at Stillington Steel Works. The run of the mill steelworks loco's though, were in abysmal condition, filthy and falling to bits, but to be fair there were exceptions, such as those at Cochrane's Cargo Fleet. The loco's had to be checked and measured for gauge i.e. nothing sticking out that would foul bridges structures etc and most importantly the wheels and tyres examined, checking that the profiles were not badly worn or flanges thin or flat.

I was soon into the busy hurly burly of this life. Collecting my time board I would stand by the door waiting for Jack to arrive, which he did eventually, being always short of breath and red in the face, but he never had any time docked!!! He would see the shop office man and get a list of loco's due for inspection and off we would go. We would walk out of the shed, catch the 'O' bus to Middlesbrough, get off near St John's Church, Marton Road and immediately fall through his terraced house front door where we would sit by a roaring coal fire (on, no matter what the time of year) and eat a large fried breakfast prepared by his wife. Then, depending which works we were going to it was another bus ride (some sort of vague pass was flashed at the conductor and they all knew him anyway) and a quick look at the loco's which were stood waiting for him. I saw some horrible sights but strangely they were always deemed to be okay for another year unless they were really, really bad (maybe the annual Christmas present in the shape of a bottle helped) and then the works foreman was always shouting and screaming when he found out it hadn't passed.

Then, bus back to St John's and a dinner by the roaring fire, his time board would be passed to me, he would set off for the pub and I would set off back to the shed giving his board in, no questions asked. I was naïve in those days!!! Later in my six months with Jack, things were even more finely tuned and we just kept our boards until the following morning so I sloped off home every day that little bit early after dinner!! To be fair I learnt a lot about wheels and tyres that stood me in good stead in later years.

Toy loco's

In 1964 I moved on to my next stage of training and actually on loco's, but not big ones!! These were in the shunting shed where Thornaby's allocation of 350hp diesel electric (class 08) and 204hp mechanical (class 03) shunters were looked after. Ward Millburn was the chargehand, with his little office at the end of the shop; he had two fitters (Dick Garbutt and Harry Maughan) an electrician (name forgotten) and John B W Smith, a fitter's mate, as his staff, though extra staff could be drafted in from the main shed if required for big jobs. The staff in the main shed always said the shunting loco staff just played with toys (!!). But there were some big heavy jobs even on such small locos.

One job that everyone disliked on the 350s was renewing the brake blocks (re-blocking). Each loco had twelve cast iron blocks, two to each wheel and these were held one above the other in split brake hangars. It was just possible for one person to lift a block, but then add standing in a pit with the brake hangars up in the air, cramped, dirty and oily conditions, hardly any room to get your hands in, you might have the picture now!! So it was a three man job to renew these blocks, one in the pit and two outside with a bar and the pins to push through the blocks, a case of gritting your teeth and getting on with it. Enter J.B. Smith, he loved doing this job because he would grab a bar and shove it in anywhere to lift the blocks up, problem was, it was just random shoving, no plan, so it usual meant your hand got jabbed or crushed by the bar. So as soon a re-block had to be done we made up some reason for J.B. to go somewhere out of the way in the hope he wouldn't find out or come back before we finished.

Of the 350hps, there were two with English Electric (EE) engine, generator and motors, D3772 and D3774 and D3138 to D3151 with Lister Blackstone engines and BTH generator and traction motors. The 350s were used for general shunting and for pushing loaded trains over the two humps in Tees Yard. Seeing the lengths of the trains that went over the humps you wouldn't expect such small locos to be able to push them, but they did. When the bad weather occurred we were often called to either of the humps to get the sands working as they relied on those sands being 100% if the rails were wet and a big load to be humped, if push came to shove (no pun intended) and the train had stalled, the yard foreman would have to get another 350hp shunter on as well.

The Lister Blackstones were a nightmare to maintain as the cylinder heads were constantly carboning up or blowing the head to liner joints out. There was always at least one stood completely stripped down. It took about a fortnight to strip one down, clean everything, grind the valves in and re-assemble. Simple jobs such as checking for fuel leaks took ages as the fuel pumps were hidden by two huge plastic covers held on by chrome channels with about 50 chrome bolts. They were nice to look at, but against the EE covers with only two knurled headed bolts which took about 30 seconds to take off there was no competition.

Jumping ahead in time when there was just a couple of Listers left in service we were having a lot of trouble with the injector pockets leaking water onto the piston crown. We had one that Ward said was definitely leaking, but a new maintenance foreman, Jimmy Dean, wasn't convinced as he wanted the loco back into service and he came down from the office to have a look. Ward had set the piston so the water was just at the bottom of the injector tube and could be seen. Along came Jim, climbed up alongside the engine and looked down the tube, "I can't see anything" he said, "bar the engine round a bit". Ward asked me to bar it round, with a whispered comment "and fast!", so I put the bar in and flicked the flywheel around as fast as I could. Of course the water had nowhere to go other than up the injector tube, which it did with great force, hit Jim under the chin knocking his head back, the water continued with such force it rose up 15 feet hit the overhead crane girder and straight back down onto Jim's head. Suffice to say he was bruised from the first whack and drenched through by the returning water, his smart clothes were ruined and he said nothing other than "Yes, there's water in there" and walked soggily back to his office. Ward just winked at me and said "Well done lad, he'll not bother us again, get that head off and a new one on". The incident was never mentioned again, but Jim kept away from the shunting shed after that.

Thornaby shunting shed 2 and 3 roads. Two BR built 204 shunters on repair. Ex steam loco tender in far end of 3 road was used as a simple load bank for testing diesels and was probably in to top the water level up.   Maurice Burns

Winter 1963/1964 provided fun and games as the shunters were left out in the yards, and come the morning there was the odd one that wouldn't start due to flat batteries. The 350hps had to be brought back to the shed for recharging whereas the Drewrys could be push started. There was a hand pump in the cab which, by vigorous pumping, could provide air to work the reverser to select the correct direction and engage second gear. Then using another loco to push or pull it only took a short distance to get the engine turning over, and one of us (usually me, being young and daft) hanging on to the open engine room door opening would hold the fuel pump throttle lever and cold start button in to get it to fire no matter how cold it was. As soon as it fired, whoever was in the cab would quickly put the gearbox into neutral otherwise the loco could accelerate away into some obstruction!! One particular morning there were that many to start, plus at least six inches of snow, so two of us went with a 204hp Drewry and a long flexible air pipe. As soon as we had hooked up to the dead loco, the air pipe was coupled between the loco's to provide air without hand pumping. In this fashion we went to Middlesbrough Docks and started three there, down to South Bank (Smith's Ship Builders) to start one, back up to Middlesbrough Goods yard to start one and finally round to Stockton Station Goods Yard to start one then back to the depot in time for dinner.

It is possible to start a 350hp loco by pushing it, but some years previously it had been banned due to someone badly burning their hand, and it was also very easy to bend the side rods. But that winter we were in dire straits for shunting loco's for the hump shunting in Tees Yard and the Shed Master gave permission to start a 350hp that had flat batteries with a push. The shunting shed electrician said he had no problems doing it as he had done it several times, so we went to the yard and borrowed a 350hp already there. The electrician explained that the trick was to use the assisting loco to sand the track up to the dead loco. Once coupled on, the electrician put the reverser into the opposite direction to that being hauled and held a traction motor contactor in with a special insulated wooden rod. I meanwhile was up on the side of the loco hanging through an open door and holding the fuel rack wide open. The hauling loco set away and within a few feet the engine started turning and fired. As soon as the engine fired the electrician dropped the contactor out and that was it, started with no fuss.

The Drewrys had lovely 8 cylinder Gardner engines which were hardly any trouble, though there was one, D2047 that had a black exhaust which we never seemed able to fix. We did everything to that engine, even stripping it down to the crankshaft and rebuilding it with all new parts; the only thing that seemed to make it reasonable was to alter the fuel pump timing so that it was advanced to far. Eventually it was due the works and when it came back with another engine of course it was okay. D2099 was another exception, it came from overhaul in the works and a few weeks later the driver using it in the yard rang up to ask us to go and look at it as there had been a bang and now it didn't seem to run right. When we arrived sure enough it was running and sounding very odd. As soon as I opened the engine room doors it was very obvious what was wrong, half the sump had been smashed away and the remains of a conn rod was whirling around. Once it was back at the shed more investigation showed that a dry liner (a shrink fit in the water cooled liner) had moved down, the piston had then jammed and sheared off letting the conn rod flail around inside the crankcase smashing through the bottom and side. So D2099 was sent back to the main works for a new engine, later it emerged that there had been a bad batch of liners supplied, as some others in that engine had come loose too.

The gearboxes on these loco's were well built but they did take a beating at times as some drivers didn't seem to have the knack of knowing when to change gear. They were however, very reliable, and on exam, the usual maintenance was to check the oil then the brake band thickness and whether the auto adjuster was working correctly. This was done using a little gauge that should just fit between two points of the mechanism. If there was any doubt then the brake band would be slackened off, then engaging the gear repeatedly should see the adjuster ratchet back until the gauge fitted. If it didn't, then it meant stripping it down and cleaning it, removing any burrs, then it usually worked okay afterwards, but don't drop anything into the gearbox as that meant taking the whole thing out, and scathing words from Ward.

Another part of the drive from the engine was the fluid flywheel. This was bolted onto the actual flywheel of the engine and was designed to absorb any transmission shocks between gearbox and engine. The flywheel was a housing three quarters full of oil, the inner surfaces had blades on them and the shaft had similar blades, as the housing rotated the oil was pushed by the outer blades onto the shaft blades thus imparting motion to the shaft. This meant that starting away, the engine revs would be higher than the shaft revs, but they would soon be the same. It was possible to have the loco brake hard on stood in gear and the engine trying to move it while the fluid flywheel took the strain. This meant that the oil would rapidly heat up, and to prevent damage there was a fusible plug fitted, which would blow, letting all the oil escape. This was a messy job to clean up as the oil went everywhere and was a job reserved for apprentices. Once cleaned, the plug would be renewed and the flywheel re-filled. The gland where the shaft came out was another source of leaks as overheating usually distorted it and the whole shaft had to be stripped down to renew that, not easy or clean jobs by any means.

I was in the shunting shed for two years whereas the norm was 6 months. Why, I never found out, but I learnt a lot in there that set me up for when I moved into the main shed. Towards the end of my time in there, we did some big jobs such as renewing a final drive on a Drewry. These were big lumps of machinery that took up the back half of the loco under the cab floor. We had done smaller repairs by lifting the top off the final drive and renewing the top layshaft and gears, but this one had to come out completely. The main works were too busy, so we set to and figured out that by using the wheel drops we could lower it out and refit a new one. It was a delicate operation that could have drastically gone wrong and there were several times when a trapped hand was a possibility, but some of the fitters from the main shed gave a hand and a few hours work saw the old one out and a new one in its place.

Another job that needed the drops was renewing the main bearings on the jackshafts; these were mounted in the mainframes and were old fashioned technology. These bearings had white metal bearing surfaces and as we still had staff skilled in that sort of thing i.e. steam loco axle boxes, it was no big deal once the bearing was out to have the coppersmith, Lenny Sherris, cast new white metal inserts into it, and Tashy Ayres, the turner, to machine them on the vertical borer.

Also in the shunting shed was a filter plant. All the main line loco's used body side filters to filter the air going into the engine room and this plant was designed to clean and re-oil them. The filters were of rectangular shape about 1 foot by 2 foot, a metal cage filled with coarse wire wool and thin straps to keep it in the cage. Obviously the loco designers knew that the maximum amount of dirt would be around the bottom of a loco body as this is where the filters were usually put, so the filters got very dirty or totally blocked.

Enter the filter plant; this consisted of a high pressure hot water section which heated the water then pumped it at high pressure through jets. It had a conveyor running through it onto which the filters were put, the conveyor moved slowly and in theory, the filters should have come out cleaned, but sometimes they had to be put through again. After that they were put in racks to drain. The next process was to dip them in a hot oil bath and then put them in a centrifuge to remove excess oil and finally stack in racks awaiting reuse. This plant wasn't modern as the operator had to keep cleaning the gunge or oil out of each machine by hand, a messy job.

The plant was manned by a fitter's assistant and it was usually the same person, Frank, every day, but occasionally a mate called Chudleigh was put on it. Chudleigh was a strange fish, which now I'm older, realise was due to his experiences in the Second World War. One day I was working on a shunter when all of a sudden there's this almighty racket from the filter plant area, so I rushed around to find the centrifuge waltzing around with a terrible din. Chudleigh was dancing around too and laughing his head off. I couldn't get to the off switch for the machine which was purely restrained from it's gyrations by the electrical conduit attached to it and the wall. The only way to stop it was to pull the main switch down that fed all the shunting shed. Once the machine stopped, Chudleigh looked most disappointed. I asked what had happened but he just grinned and shook his head. I peered in the centrifuge to find that he had only loaded one of four arms with filters so the thing was totally out of balance, no wonder it took off. Another fitter and I barred the poor thing back into position and the DOME renewed the floor bolts and it worked perfectly when next used. They made things to last in those days!

Free Passes

One of the perks of the job, but I suppose one of the reasons why the railway pay was so low in comparison to outside jobs was free passes or privilege tickets. After a year in the job I was eligible to a few free passes and a form had to be filled in stating from where to where and the office upstairs would write out a ticket by the following day. Being a train spotter in those days this was the opportunity to travel distances I had previously only dreamt of. There were other train spotters in the apprentice ranks and a couple of times I went with Lenny Johnston to the Isle of Wight to catch the O2 tanks working there before they disappeared. We also went twice to the Talyllyn railway from London Paddington, hauled by a GWR Castle class. A marathon trip was two weeks travelling around all the Scottish sheds and works with Peter Tuck. This needed careful planning on what the free pass wording was, to get the maximum distance and destinations from one pass. Some of the ticket collectors and guards would study the pass and purse their lips but we never got chucked off the train. Luckily we had a Scottish shedmaster at that time and he was very useful in getting us the necessary permits for all sheds and main works. Though for some reason we couldn't get a permit for St Rollox, Glasgow but we took a chance and went anyway, flashing the permit for the other works got us in!! Trips to Manchester and Crewe followed, after all, what else could the passes and privilege tickets be used on?

Three cold 37s having just started up in the bull ring, note very smoky exhausts
Dick Watson

Main depot

At last, in 1965, I was in the main shed and learning about Sulzer type 2s and EE type 3s. Thornaby had a large allocation of both types by then, plus a couple of EE type 4s, and my first few months were spent working with the fitters and doing examinations. These went from B exams up to E exams (the A exam being a weekly running check). There was a lot to learn, as even within the same type of loco there were differences in where certain items were, or even different types of filters. There were little traps as well that meant a lesson learnt the hard way. On the type 3s the majority had a lub oil filter made by 'Hilco'. This comprised two vertical tubes in which there were three filter elements each, the top lid was held on by three wing nuts, also in the lid was a small bleed screw. The purpose of the bleed screw was firstly to let air in to drain the oil out, which took several hours, then when the engine was started, to let the air out. So on the exam sheets would be written the comment 'Lub oil filters to bleed, vents left open'. You can see that it was easy to forget this simple comment and start the engine and forget about the vents, the net result being that within a few minutes the engine room was awash with lub oil. I only did that once as it was a messy laborious task cleaning the mess up!!

In late 1965 we had had a really wet weekend and whilst working in the main shed we heard a loud muffled bang which came from the direction of the 'bullring' (Roundhouse with a turntable) so we all rushed in to see a Type 3 standing on one of the roads with smoke pouring out of one of the cab doors, and a driver staggering towards us holding his head. It turned out that the driver had gone to start the engine, and unbeknown to him, the loco had been stood all weekend with one of the exhaust ports underneath a broken rain gutter, so the engine had part filled up with water. As soon as the driver pushed the start button the engine had rotated so far then hydrauliced, i.e. the first piston heading to top dead centre had hit the water and compressed it against the cylinder head. But water doesn't compress, so the effect was like hitting a brick wall. It had broken the cylinder head studs, smashed the piston and bent the crankshaft, also the main generator had burnt the start windings out, as the driver for some reason in the shock of it all had kept his finger on the start button. A driver who had been nearby swore that the whole loco had jumped up in the air about a foot!!!

Replacing a piston into a class 31 'English Electric' engine   Phil Thickett

Boiling water

After six months of exams I was put with 'Budgie' Dawson (yes he kept budgies as a hobby), I never knew his real Christian name. Budgie was the fitter who dealt with train heating boilers. In 1965/66 most diesels had train heating boilers fitted so even though Thornaby was a depot that only dealt with freight train working, some of its loco's had boilers and they had to be kept in working condition. So there were two types of boilers to look after. The type 3s had 'Clayton' boilers and the type 2s had 'Stones' boilers, and whilst both had a double coil of steel pipe inside a metal casing, their operating systems were not alike at all. The simple principle was that the coil sat above a nozzle through which fuel was pumped, atomising in the process, and ignited by an electrical spark. A fan also blew air through and the resulting fire ball went through the coil and up until eventually exhausting through a vent in the roof. Water was pumped in at one end of the coil and due to the intense heat had mostly turned to steam by the time it reached the other end. A small reservoir was connected to the output end of the coil and this collected the steam and at the same time the

TAKING THE WEIGHT

small amount of water that passed through, so that the main take off at the top passed only dry steam. As the steam pressure reached maximum the automatic controls reduced the amount of fuel and also the water passing through the coil until just before the safety valves operated the fuel and water were switched off. Sounds fool proof doesn't it??

These boilers had been designed a long time ago and been brought to perfection over the years. There were thousands and thousands, so we were told, around the world, working in laundries, hotels, on ships, anywhere a plentiful supply of steam or very hot water was required. But stick it in a railway loco and that was its death knell. Budgie struggled all day everyday keeping those things going and he knew them inside out, being mainly self-taught, as training courses had told him they were reliable and would never go wrong.

You name it and it went wrong, transformers for increasing the voltage for the spark across the electrodes burnt out, electrodes fell to bits, water pumps seized up or seals blew out, motors burnt out, control boxes fell apart, the list was endless. So I spent all my time figuring out why it wouldn't work, then if it wasn't obvious, changing something to see if that would cure it. Personally I liked the 'Claytons' as you could see what was happening and they were relatively simple, whereas a 'Stones' had a secret life of its own, seemed over complicated, and had a gadget called a butterfly that looked like a ginormous bow tie. This would turn one way or the other in its efforts to control the proportion of water to fuel burnt and had too many settings to alter and get wrong. There were also a lot more valves to twiddle, get them in the wrong order and you were sunk. Luckily I didn't have much to do with the Stones as there weren't many of them. There were also Spanner boilers but it was very rare to see one of them at Thornaby and I didn't come across them until much later when I was a Supervisor.

The 'Spanner Boilers' had three variants, a MK1 which was a large vertical boiler with a firebox at the bottom where the fuel burner was mounted, the fuel pump was driven off the fan motor and tubes carried the heat through the water and then out through a roof exhaust. Two 'Mobray' float switches kept the water level in tolerance by switching the water pump on and off and there was even a gauge glass to check where the level was!!!

A pressure switch dealt with switching the combined fuel pump fan motor on and off according to the pressure settings, and finally two safety valves. What could be simpler being based on steam engine technology?? From an empty boiler, steam could be raised in about 20 minutes (whereas a Clayton or Stones could raise steam from cold in less than 4 minutes). The MK2 had a much smaller boiler that was mounted horizontally, but still used a similar control system to the MK1, higher fuel pressure and different nozzles gave a higher steam output even though the boiler was smaller in size. The MK3 was virtually the same as the MK2 with different settings to give an even greater output. These two boilers could raise steam from empty in about 5 minutes. Being an early design, the MK1s were fitted to the Class 31s, the MK2s to Deltics and class 47s and the MK3s to later build 47s. All three makes, Clayton, Spanner and Stones were fitted to the class 47s as BR had to follow the edict of the government of the time that orders had to be shared amongst several manufacturing firms no matter which was the cheapest or most reliable.

One job Budgie hated was acid washing the coils, which had to be done every so often to remove the sludge and scale that built up inside them, otherwise the coil would overheat and burn out. This entailed disconnecting the boiler coil from the rest of the pipework, as the rest of the boiler didn't like acid, and connecting flexible pipes to each end of the coil pipe work. The flexible pipes went through the loco access hatch to a medieval machine on wheels that had a large tank of water and an electrically driven pump, the whole thing looking like it had come from the ark. Once the pump was running, the water was allowed to circulate through the boiler coil until all the air was displaced, then a carefully measured amount of acid powder (the type escapes me after all these years) was added to the tank. Within minutes the discharge pipe was pouring a frothy murky liquid back into the tank. This went on for several hours until it subsided and another smaller measure of powder was added, this was repeated until the discharge ran clear and everything could be disconnected and put back to normal. Of course Budgie wore protective clothing, i.e. his normal overalls and a battered pair of heavy duty gloves, as he said "the acid splashes only burn for a short time". What I could never understand was that every coil washout always entailed overtime for Budgie, even though some took no time at all to run clear as being freight loco's the boilers probably hadn't worked much, if at all, but then I suppose the budgies at home had to be fed.

Being machines that were very erratic we had some fun with them, or should I say, them with us, A type 3 had had a B exam and was on final run up in the straight shed 10 road, so Budgie and I went to test the 'Clayton' boiler. This entailed running the boiler up from cold to operating pressure, which only took a few minutes then opening a buffer beam cock and seeing what pressure it could maintain against this large demand and not run out of water. This of course filled the shed with steam. Budgie would then rapidly shut the main isolating cock in the engine room so that the steam pressure would rise quickly as the burner was still full on, thus beating the control system, and the safety valves would open, the pressure being noted for the records. Of course Budgie had forgotten the loco was in the shed under a glass roof!! Suffice to say 10 road had quite a few panes of glass missing for a few weeks; luckily nobody was standing where they fell, and boilers were always tested outside after that.

Then we had a 'Clayton' that suffered from excess fuel at the nozzles, it had been reported as making too much steam and blowing off continually and even a report of a glow in the sky from one driver, which Budgie dismissed as fantasy. So as it was outside, we ran the boiler and had the buffer beam cock wide open and that boiler made steam like no other we had seen, but apart from that it was okay. Then someone came by and said the telephones from the cabin across the way had gone off and it looked like the overhead wires had been cut and had we seen anything happen. "No" we said and looked up at our loco. Just then a dark cloud came over revealing a three foot diameter blowtorch erupting six feet into the air from the boiler exhaust where the wires had once been. So the driver's report of a glow had been true, but we couldn't understand why no signal box had reported it during the night. The problem was that the fuel pressure relief valve had failed allowing the fuel pressure to be more than twice what it should have been.

The next incident was along similar lines but the report was 'Won't make enough steam'. I went on and checked everything over, no fault being apparent, and then I started the boiler up. It fired up and seemed ok, the pressure built up and the burners shut down. Once the pressure dropped the burners didn't light up again so I tried a few things then lay on the floor to see if there was a spark at the electrodes. As I did, I noticed neat fuel running out of the burner housing. Getting up to switch the boiler off, I was too late, the burners ignited and took the excess fuel with it, there was a loud whooomph, the exhaust stack lifted off the boiler top, and I stood there covered from head to foot in a thick sticky black soot. Budgie came running because of the noise and just sat there and laughed and laughed. It took me ages to get clean after that.

Hair cut

Of course, having a number of apprentices meant there was fun and games all the time. Those that come to mind were, being careful to make sure your overalls back strap was always left undone, otherwise if walking by a crane you could find yourself suddenly being hoisted in the air by the strap. Getting your shoe toes painted white as you worked on the side of a loco by someone in the pit was another, as was getting drenched by a water hose that just happened to be aimed your way. Things could go to extremes though. Alan Trodden had long curly hair down to his shoulders and some of the apprentices thought it would be fun to give him a haircut one afternoon. Alan got wind of this and hid, but they found him, he escaped and ran like the wind with them giving chase. The chase went all around the shed and out into Tees Yard where eventually he was cornered in a guards van and a blunt pair of scissors used to trim just one side of his precious locks. So he had to go home on the train with half his hair missing in a ragged fashion. Next day he turned up, hair very short all round and he kept it that way for the rest of his time at Thornaby.

All Bells and Horns

My next move took me onto the Automatic Warning Systems (AWS) with Eric Ayres and William (surname forgotten), another pair of gentlemen. William was a lay preacher at a chapel in Stockton and hated the swearing and things that were at locomotive depots, but never pushed his religion at anyone. The AWS was a reliable system and though there were faults they were soon put right. Eric and William had built a test unit in their little office and any suspect component would be placed in the unit to see if it was faulty. Otherwise they were to be seen heading for a loco with a hand magnet on a long pole for swinging under the AWS receiver mounted under the bogie, and the green steel test box that enabled the AWS system to be tested on the loco, the test box usually found any problem. All the components were sealed so we couldn't strip them down or repair them, they had to be sent away and replacements obtained from the stores. Another task that fell to them was fire bottles. All the loco fixed fire systems and cab hand extinguishers had to be examined at fixed examination periods and a crucial part of this was checking the levels. To do this there was an instrument kept in a lead lined box (!) which had a radio active isotope mounted at one end of a hoop arrangement and a radiation detector at the other end. By passing the two ends up and down the exterior of the bottle and watching a needle gauge it was possible to detect where the level of the liquid in the fire bottle was as the needle deflected at that point and a chalk mark made. As well as a hazard sign on the box there also had to be a sign on the office door where the box was kept in a signed locked locker, and obviously only certified persons were allowed to use that test box.

Haunted

Not sure of the year in the mid 60's but I arrived at work and found out that there had been an accident to a driver the previous day and the loco was in quarantine in the bull ring. What had happened was that D6769 (eventually 37069) had been heading to York and driver J Potter had swapped places with his secondman after they had passed Thirsk. As Potter sat in the secondman's seat a Deltic hauled passenger train passed on the opposite line and a lump of metal smashed through the windscreen severely injuring driver Potter on the head. The secondman stopped the train at the next signal and informed the signalman. The train was then moved to a road over bridge where driver Potter was taken by ambulance to York hospital, where unfortunately he died. D6769 was removed from the train and hauled back to Thornaby for investigation. It transpired that a brake shoe guide on one of the bogies of the Deltic had broken off just as it passed D6769 at 100mph, hit a sleeper and ricochet up and through the secondman's windscreen, a million to one chance of several events combining together to cause a tragedy. Once the cause had been established D6769 was released by the police and a shed labourer was sent into the cab to clean up. The windscreen was renewed and the loco sent back into traffic and that should have been the end of it.

While the loco was sat in the bullring a fitter on nights was working near it and came racing into the main shed swearing blind he had seen a shadowy figure climb out of 69's cab. He couldn't be persuaded to go back in the bull ring that night. Thereafter 69's history was littered with strange happenings being attributed to it being haunted. I worked on the loco several times and must admit there was a strange feel to it!!!

The guide that had broken off the Deltic was a feature on class 37 bogies as well, so a campaign check was immediately done on all the bogies and several guides were found to have fractured welds. This caused a design change which was done as the loco's went through main works for overhaul, and we had to make sure these guides were checked every time an EE type 3 came on the depot until all had been modified.

Much later, when depots were having loco's named after the home depot, and we wanted to do the same, once permission was granted, D6769, now numbered 37069, was chosen to carry the name Thornaby TMD in honour of driver Potter, the name being carried from September 1986.

37069 when it was named 'Thornaby TMD' 29th September 1986.
Note the amount of 'Bulling up' done on locos when named.   D Hudspeth

Heads and Liners

My last couple of years were spent doing heavy work on loco's, cylinder heads, pistons and liners. This was heavy strenuous work, using a large torque wrench to pull cylinder head nuts down to 900 ft/Lbs and was no joke, especially when you ended up hanging over the edge of the body side and still pulling for all your worth. By then we had an allocation of Sulzer type 4s as well as an increase in EE type 4s and there was plenty of variety in the work.

One summer morning we were sat outside the main shed having a well earned breather when we saw an EE type 4 coming into the yard with intermittent puffs of white exhaust coming from the stacks. Even more noticeable was the noise the loco was making as it drew opposite it us. A description of a washing machine full of scrap bits of metal gone wrong is about the nearest we could come up with. Eventually it came onto the shed and the driver had booked engine noisy and low power. The fitter on running repairs shut it down and let it cool off before removing the crankcase doors. After a good look round, he went to the Supervisor saying he wasn't sure but could someone with a bit more knowledge have a look at it. It transpired that the crankshaft had broken in two halfway along its length and in the middle of a bearing, so only the back half of the engine was actually running properly and driving the generator, the front half sort of ran but going in or out of phase with the engine timing, thus did or didn't fire and the valves took a beating from the pistons, but it kept going against all the odds. I seem to remember the English Electric rep coming and saying it was impossible, and anyway their crankshafts didn't break in two.

Them and Us

In those days there were fitters and electricians and never the twain would meet. It was apparent from day one of the diesels that there were some strange laws operating. A nasty job was changing a triple pump on a Sulzer or BRCW type 2, as whoever had designed the loco's had not given any thought at all as to how this pump would be changed when the loco was in service. He couldn't have put it in a more impossible place if he had tried, though to be fair when they placed it into a Sulzer type 4 they did manage to find an even worse place. Basically the triple pump was a large electric motor with a coolant pump mounted at one end and a fuel and lub oil pump at the other end. To my knowledge we never had any problems with the actual pumps but the motors would burn out. So what happened was that the electrician would come along all nice and clean, spend ten minutes uncoupling the two wires and the flexible conduit and then go off whistling. Then a fitter and his mate (or apprentice) would go in, uncouple all the pipe work then the mounting bolts (which were nasty things to get at) and then struggle for a long time to get the heavy lump up from a small pit let into the floor beneath the blower motor, raise it up into the air so it could then be slid along bits of timber into the cab (the door into the cab being just ½" wider than the pump) then to the cab door (don't damage the floor lads, driver likes a nice floor) for the crane to lift it down. Apart from working on the engine through roof doors there was no means of lifting inside engine rooms other than pure body strength, no cranes or anything like that. So that was 4 hours hard graft, then another 4 hours getting the new one in place and the pipes coupled up. Yes you've guessed, along comes the electrician, whistling, 10 minutes to couple the flexible conduit and two wires and he's finished. This was something wrong to my way of thinking, as it was the motor that was at fault, but demarcation was rife.

I can remember one loco where unfortunately (!) the triple pump managed to crush the wires and conduit as it was put into its little pit. The fitter was heard to say "Oh dear, never mind" and the electrician's face was a picture when he came to couple it up, because now he was on his hands and knees sweating and getting dirty having to repair the conduit in a difficult place. It's a big pity that designers in those days never had to work on their wonderful creations. They managed to perform wonders cramming everything into a small place, so neat and tidy but never any consideration for the poor fitter or electrician who had to maintain or repair it when all the pieces were in the body. Things have improved greatly since with the class 60s and especially the American class 66 loco's being lovely to work on, but even they have parts that are awkward to get at.

With the sparkies

Though I was an apprentice fitter I was given some time to be with the electricians where they tried to pass on some knowledge of what was happening with all these wires and motors and how to read electrical schematics. Ernie Pinkney taught me a useful trick when we were trying to find a fault on the lighting of a Sulzer type 2 which was blowing the fuse straight away; we had checked every bit of the lighting visually so he took the fuse out and put in its place a bent six inch nail. Switching on all the lights he sat in the cab and proceeded to roll a cigarette. "Just walk round and round the cabs and outside" he said "while I rest here and think". So always doing as I was told, I did. Sure enough ten minutes later I spotted a pillar of smoke coming from a tail lamp housing where a faulty light fitting was in the process of melting down. I was assured this was a sure fire way of finding short circuits!! Working with the electricians gave me an insight into reading schematics and fault finding that I could expand upon and it proved very useful in the years to come.

Whilst with the electricians they took advantage of having an apprentice with them, so all the dirty jobs came my way. Traction motor brush changes were dirty jobs no matter which class of loco. Changing brushes on a type 2 main generator was really hard work as the bottom brushes were just within reach of a stretched out arm, grovelling around underneath the generator and purely feeling what I was doing with my fingertips as there was no chance of seeing anything. Later generators were slightly better as the brush arms which held the brushes could be rotated round so the bottom ones became visible.

Centre cab nightmare

In the late 1960's a strange looking loco rolled onto the depot, it had a centre cab with a low bonnet at each end. This was a 'Clayton' type 1, designed by the Clayton Equipment Company and built by Beyer Peacock & Co of Gorton Manchester, ordered, as so many early diesels for B.R. straight from the drawing board. The design ethos was sound in that the central cab driving position gave the driver an excellent view all round, and the cab was big enough to hold a dance in!!! The reason for the large cab was that it had been planned to put a train heating boiler smack in the centre, but luckily for the drivers this never happened. (The thought of one of those hot hissing lumps of machinery taking up most of the cab and leaking steam and diesel fuel all over didn't bear thinking about). So a counterweight to keep the loco weight correct was installed under the cab floor instead. The drivers loved these loco's; they rode smoothly, had comfortable cabs which weren't too draughty and as mentioned previously, had very good visibility. A good point with them was that the electrical system had a selector switch whereby the driver, if an engine failed, could isolate it out and use the remaining one to power either just two motors or four motors or any combination of motors from two engines, which was just as well considering what was to come. These loco's had been built too late though as the work they were designed for had virtually disappeared. These had been the local trip workings and yard to yard transfers, plus at only 900hp they weren't strong enough for anything else so they were seen in multiple on bigger trains to get some use out of them, but some locations with head shunts were a bit tight for the room needed to get the length of two loco's in, so their future was in doubt before they were built.

The design policy of straight off the drawing board dealt the fateful blow. The loco's had basic flaws, the main one being the 'Paxman' engines they were fitted with. These engines were of 450hp each, six cylinders but in a flat configuration, the reason they had been chosen, as they would fit under the low bonnet. This meant the cylinders were horizontal instead of the normal vertical design. Within the first few months the major faults began to show; firstly the cylinder head to block joints started to fail. The heads were an aluminium alloy casting and these slowly distorted and the torque setting of the head nuts eased off allowing the heads to move and leak. Heads blowing and leaking coolant became rife; the 'Paxman' engineers tried everything, from special nuts and washers to different studs with collars, but to no avail. So they returned to the good old trusted design of cast iron heads, and the joint failures stopped. This change of design came at a price though. Firstly, the engine was now a lot heavier, and secondly, the engines had to go back to 'Paxmans' for modification. Step into the breech Bill Glaves. Bill had come to Thornaby when Darlington Works had closed down so had experience of heavy work like this. But to us he had a reputation for dodging difficult jobs and it was a complete surprise when he took on the job of changing engines with the 'Paxman' engineers, but perhaps the guaranteed 7 days a week with overtime helped him make the decision. By using the 7 ½ ton drops crane there was just enough headroom to firstly remove the bonnet, then the engine and place them on a spare low wagon, and as the renovated engines came by rail, a process of shuttling things up and down under the crane enabled the engine changes to take place fairly easily, it taking two days to complete a loco.

Great, we all thought, new engines, problems solved, we can relax, but oh no, the next Achilles heel soon appeared, oil leaks. These 'Paxman' engines used 'O' rings at virtually every pipe joint and sure enough every joint started to leak. Being 'O' rings they couldn't be tightened so the 'O' ring had to be renewed. Of course some of the joints were nigh on impossible to get to, and my speciality because of my height and slim build, was the elbow between the block and sump. The elbow was under the engine so I had to slide myself into the gap between the engine and sealing floor plate, which was just possible even for me. This meant every one of these joints that needed doing was my job; no one else could get in. It wasn't easy working in such a confined place with your head tilted to one side, arms above your head and usually a screaming hot engine above you. Despite all our best efforts these engines leaked oil continually and the running shed was set up on one road specifically for these loco's so that when one came in we could completely refill the coolant tank, engine sump and the Hydrostatic system tanks as quickly as possible, as it was guaranteed that any 'Clayton' coming in would be empty. If there was a redeeming feature it was the choice of 'Crompton Parkinson' for the electrical system and machines. They gave hardly any trouble, which was just as well as most of them were permanently oil cooled. These loco's could always be spotted from a distance as they usually had a dirty exhaust from at least one engine. This was due to either the fuel pumps losing their setting as the flexible drives to them kept coming loose and eventually falling apart, or the flat design of engine contributing to heavy wear of the pistons and their rings, so a lot of oil was being burnt. Again 'Paxman' put a lot of energy into solving these problems but never came up with a solution that worked. As with the boilers, these engines worked fine in static or boat situations but stick them in a loco and they were doomed.

Six months at Doncaster Works 1967

Until the late 1980s all locomotives and coaches were given major overhauls at a regional workshop, in my case Doncaster (The Plant), and all Eastern Region apprentices in their last year of apprenticeship had to go there for six months training to get an insight into the heavier maintenance they did. Alan Trodden, though nearly a year my junior, was also nominated to go at the same time. I had never been away from home before so it was with some trepidation we both set off from Middlesbrough station early one November morning. We had to report to the chief clerk's office at 08.00 prompt and once there we found ourselves with several other apprentices from other Eastern depots. Led into see the man himself, (a stern man who obviously would brook no trouble), we were given a long lecture on what we could, or more properly, could not do. Before leaving the office we were allocated lodgings in Doncaster, (these were run by ex-works employees who appreciated a bit of extra money) and finally given a timetable of where we would be during our six months in the works.

No time was given to get our bearings or find our lodgings as we were all dispatched to our allotted places, overalls on and set to work. The works were a completely different world to that of the depots. Depots had a human side to them, not Doncaster!! In the works, anyone above charge hand were, to us, inhuman and dictatorial, no latitude given in anything whatsoever, especially apprentices from depots, we were the lowest of the low, if not lower. Starting and finishing times were precise at all times and the lavatory attendant would report anyone to the foreman who was in a cubicle for more than five minutes. Each shop had a raised office that could oversee the whole shop; this office was the foreman's who passed his orders down to the charge hands, the charge man having a tall desk and stool to do his paperwork on.

At the end of this first shift, in what at the time seemed like hell to us, Alan and I made our way out of the works over the footbridge that crossed the station and had to find our way to our lodgings. Armed with only a scrap of paper with a scribbled address on it and very brief instructions we eventually found the right bus stop and set off into the unknown. Eventually we stood outside a pre-war council house and timidly knocked on its door. After a long time it was opened by an old lady who welcomed us in, her husband was a retired fitter from the plant and her son was a clerk in the plant also. Accommodation was basic but clean, the meals were sufficient but never varied at all, and we ate with them. Being winter it was very cold and the tiny bedroom with its two small beds was freezing all the time, no heating in there. In the mornings we were given our bait boxes which had the same meal in every day, an apple, piece of cheese and one slice of buttered bread. It didn't take us long to decide to pay for lunch in the works canteen where the meals were hot, varied and very good quality.

We soon fell into the pattern of life there and occasionally managed to escape the lodgings to the town, with the proviso we were back in by 9.30 as the front door would be locked then!! Towards the end of our time at Doncaster, one Monday morning just after we had arrived there, Alan and I were summoned to the chief clerk's office to be met by the landlady's son who told us his father had died during that weekend but that we would still be lodging there. After work we, again with trepidation, went to the front door, she opened it and said "Come in, but be quiet as he's in the front room". Sure enough there was the coffin, which we had to squeeze by to get upstairs. She just carried on as usual then and after the funeral, as if nothing had happened.

It would be an understatement to say Alan and I hated every minute at Doncaster (I still grimace every time I go through that station on a train). But a saviour appeared in the form of college. It took a while and some letters from my college and our shed master explaining that I was coming up to my final exams, and swapping colleges to Doncaster wouldn't be good for my results.

My weekly timetable now was:

Monday to Doncaster and finish at 4.30pm to lodgings

Tuesday finish at 3pm train home for night school

Wednesday to Doncaster start at 10am finishing at 4.30 train home

Thursday at college all day in Middlesbrough

Friday to Doncaster start at 10am finishing at 3pm train home

So I wasn't there that much at all, despite the efforts of the Doncaster chief clerk to get me to do college at Doncaster.

My first shop was the DMU shop; there all the Eastern Diesel Multiple Units had their major overhauls or damage repaired. At that time there were a lot of different types of DMU in service and having never worked on any before there was a lot to learn. As was to be expected, there was a lot of demarcation lines in the shops and I was allocated to the 'Willis' gang. This constituted a working charge hand (obviously called Willis!), two fitters, two mates, a labourer and two apprentices. Each gang was given a unit to overhaul from start to finish, and it was planned so that on a Monday it was a fresh vehicle and hopefully by Friday afternoon shop the vehicle would be finished so the shop was empty over the weekend. So on Monday we would go in, disconnect the bogies, get the overhead cranes, lift the body up and roll the bogies out, lowering the body onto stands. The bogies were taken away for refurbishment in another shop as were all the other components we removed, engines, gearboxes, control gear brakes, components etc. Once everything was removed the underframe was thoroughly cleaned with high pressure hot water and chemicals and then checked for damage and fractures. All components would then be replaced with any modifications being done at the same time. The main one while I was there was the fitting of safety straps to prop shafts, gearboxes and engines, this mod being required after a spate of gearboxes and prop shafts falling down.

There was a small gang in the shop whose whole purpose in life was drilling holes, we would mark out all the holes required and then have to go and book a driller to come and do the actual drilling. A bit of planning here meant we could nip up into the coach for a short time, sitting on the floor out of sight of the chargeman. Whilst all the work was going on the painters would either be patching up or doing partial repaints. I don't know how they managed to achieve the excellent results they did given the dusty dirty conditions they worked in.

When all was complete the body was lifted again and bogies rolled into place, then once lowered the bogies were recoupled and final checks made of all the work before we pushed the vehicle outside for testing. This was done outside in a test shop so the fumes and noise wouldn't affect the main shop. Of course the gang did the testing as well, so a full day was spent checking all the systems in fine detail and all results recorded neatly on to test sheets.

The shop overhauled the 'Hull' cross country sets; these DMUs had power cars in the middle of the sets and therefore no cabs. To test these, a console on castors was provided by simply using the multiple jumpers and sockets. One day we were stripping a unit down and a lot of shouting alerted us to the fact a Hull unit was moving in the test house and accelerating down the track dragging the console behind it. The fitter was trying to stop it but it kept going until eventually the cable connector snapped and it ground to a halt. No one was hurt except the fitter's pride as he had left the final drives engaged while testing the gearboxes. The console was a lot worse for the experience and had to be repaired in the shop by the gang that had wrecked it. This was the first time I had come across tool banging; anytime something went wrong, immediately all the staff nearby would bang spanners or hammers on anything that would make a loud noise, so the banging would rapidly spread through the whole shop and people would come running to see what had happened.

After the DMU shop I spent a fortnight in the turbo charger shop where all turbos of various types were overhauled and repaired. This was fun, as the fitter I was with hardly said a word and wouldn't let me touch a spanner or anything! So for a fortnight I watched him strip a turbo down and clean all the bits in a caustic bath. Occasionally he was really kind, and I could wash the bits with hot water. He would then examine the parts, renewing as necessary, re-assemble and spin test. All this was done in perfect silence, turbo after turbo. I suppose I learnt something.

The next move was to the compressor shop. Here all shapes and sizes of compressor and exhausters were dealt with, being stripped down to the last nut and bolt, put back together and tested. I was placed with a Polish fitter who I had difficulty in understanding, but he certainly knew his stuff. When the compressor was completed it was lifted onto a steel table, 110v power cables attached via crocodile clips and switched on. This was to prove everything was in balance as it shouldn't move on the plate, and then be left running for an hour to bed the bearings in. Seeing the Polish fitter hanging on to a gyrating class 37 compressor whilst trying to stop it throwing itself onto the floor, and yelling "Switch it off!", proved that things sometimes did go wrong. Once the bearings had been checked the compressor was coupled to the works air supply and left working for half an hour on load. As long as the bearings were again okay it was given an oil change, sealed, and sent to the stores.

My next move was to the 'Crimpsall', this was the main workshop of the works where all locomotives were overhauled or repaired. As usual I started on the shunters, learning a lot more as I helped rebuild a 350 shunter, then a Drewry from bare frames to it being driven out of the shop for completion of the painting. Whilst in that shop one afternoon, there was an almighty bang, then complete silence as everyone looked around. After a few more seconds the spanner banging started until every shop was ringing with the sound. I went into the next bay where collision damage repairs were carried out, to find a class 31 in a cloud of dust with several staff looking at it. The overhead cranes had been in the process of lifting the body off its stands, and a lifting bracket had become loose allowing the body to drop several feet. Luckily the loco had dropped back exactly onto the stands.

Unfortunately, I never had chance to work on the Deltics which by then had all overhauls and repairs done at Doncaster in the main shop called the 'Crimpsall', including the engines. The engines had, until recently, been overhauled at the English Electric factory under the initial contract. The 'Crimpsall' didn't have enough height to lift the engines in and out so BR had to spend some money and provide a deep pit into which the loco body was lowered to achieve the head room required.

I spent most of my time working with the gang that were re-engining the class 31s from Mirrilees to English Electric engines and several other modifications. One of these was to fit pipework for a cooling air supply from the traction motor blower system to the automatic voltage regulator (AVR) which tended to overheat. This involved running a 2½" diameter pipe from the blower ducting, up through the floor to the base of the AVR and a flexible hose completed the job. I would mark out where the hole was required under the floor then go and find a driller. In this bay it was an old chap who carried a huge old air drill with various drill and extension rods so that the drill could be set up in any situation. Then came the day he came to drill this 2½" hole for me, all in one go. Halfway through drilling, the drill jammed solid and the air drill started to revolve, despite the efforts of the driller to stop it, as the trigger had jammed. Eventually he gave up and we all found something to sit on to watch as the machine slowly purred round and round winding the air hose around itself. Once the hose was totally wrapped around it, then it proceeded to rip the fixed air pipe off the wall until the stress snapped the pipe with a bang, which of course resulted in more spanner banging!! No quick release valves or handy isolation valves in those days.

Bad news travels fast on the railway, so an hour after it happened we all knew about the collision involving DP2 at Thirsk on 31st July 1967 where several people had been killed and the loco badly damaged. It wasn't until I got home on the Friday night that I learnt that my brother had been on the train with a friend, travelling in the first coach (in which the deaths occurred) but five minutes before the crash they had gone to the buffet car in the middle of the train which didn't even derail!!

My last few weeks were spent with a fitter who sorted out any faults on ex works loco's that had failed on their trial run or been returned for rectification from the depot. This was interesting work ranging from repairing a sliding cab window on a class 37, faulty heaters, finding a bad knock on a Mirrilees engine, to re-setting a fuel pump on a Paxman type 1 D8401. This was a nightmare job on a badly designed engine (oops Paxman again!) where the fuel pump was situated in the vee of the engine between the exhaust pipes.

At last the 6 months was over and on our last day after enduring a grilling - sorry interview - with the works manager, another very fearsome character, they let us all go an hour early!!

Last apprentice days

On my return from Doncaster works I only had a few months to go before I was out of my time (apprenticeship completed) and things looked grim. I received a letter saying there were no places available for me at Thornaby so the future looked bleak for a railway career. Joe I'anson the NUR union rep then stepped into the picture. He had spotted that there was a spare position on the books that was purposely being left unfilled and went to see the shedmaster. So various wheels moved and I quickly received another letter saying I would be appointed as a fitter at Thornaby on the 6th May 1968.

A V2 on the 5 road wheeldrops, the 6 road wheeldrops are just in view (left foreground).
Maurice Burns

Prior to that day arriving, I was thrown into the hurly burly of heavy work with Frankie Kidd, he was also the lead fitter on the tool vans and eventually became Breakdown Supervisor at March TMD. Whilst I was with him, Frank pioneered the changing of wheelsets and traction motors on the wheel drops, which with a few modifications to equipment and procedures, remained in use until the depot closed.

The first loco to go on the drops was D1777 which had suffered a seized T/Motor bearing and it took us a week to get the wheelset out!! This involved a very steep learning curve and the making of various tools and fittings. We asked the main works, in this case Crewe, for advice but they refused as we were stealing their work! Eventually the CMEE at York managed to get us a set of 'Brush' maintenance manuals which showed how to remove the various bolts from metalistic bushes in the equalising beams and T/Motor suspension links. So Frank made special extractors which were used for years to come.

Once the wheelset was free of the bogie the next problem was getting the wheelset under the drops crane. Thornaby had a complicated arrangement

TAKING THE WEIGHT

of tunnels that linked two sets of drops. At the set of drops on 5 road the table went down to the bottom and the wheelset was pushed off and along a tunnel onto a table that was moved along a hundred yards where the wheelset could be lifted up to the top by a 7½ ton crane and placed on 4 road (or the wheel lathe if steam loco wheels). The second set of drops on 6 road was a oddity, the table went down and then the top of the table complete with the rails the wheels were on could be moved sideways 12 feet to line up with the previously mentioned table track from 5 road drops to get to the crane. All the tables had to be manually moved by hand cranking which was a hard back breaking task, and if they jammed, needed a big bar or even a winch to get it moving again. As you can see, the wheelsets were manhandled from table to table, which if the T/Motor was seized, wasn't an easy matter.

As the traction motor was attached to the axle, Frank had to figure out how to support the motor. After much head scratching we obtained a set of small plate layers' trolley wheels and fastened them to the traction motor with brackets. Using 12 ton Pul-Lifts the seized wheelset was slid from table to table and eventually hoisted up with the crane. Removing and replacing the traction motor was an easy, straight forward job, and now the assembly could be pushed along the tracks. Getting them back into the bogie was also easy as we had learnt a lot in taking them out!

Once D1777 was completed and successfully back in traffic we got a steady flow of wheelsets or traction motors to change as it was a lot cheaper for us to do it than send to the main works. So we had to figure out how to do this with each class of loco, each being different. The class 40 – 45 and 46 were the worst because all the work had to be done in really filthy dirty condition, and in a confined space.

As the years passed and experience grew, better tools were available, and a very low small thin trolley made to support the traction motor, the time taken to change anything on the drops became shorter, so a wheelset could be changed in 12 hours. When better designed loco's came along as in the American built class 66 it was commonplace to have at least two if not three wheelsets removed and replaced in a twelve hour shift.

College

When I left College at Darlington I enrolled at Longlands Technical College, Middlesbrough. I'm not sure why, but probably going from my results obtained at Darlington, I ended up on a Technician's course. This was a four year course with Part 1 obtained after year two, and Part 2 after the four years. Part 2 was taken at the then brand new Polytechnic on Borough Road, Middlesbrough (now part of Teesside University).

As I couldn't see any correlation between the course work and my apprenticeship, it was a bit boring at times, but I'm sure the training on lathes etc. and metallurgy has come in useful. The last six months were hell, as the maths lecturer hounded me, and I'll be the first to say, maths isn't my strong point, a bit like PE really. I can remember walking into the maths exam room with trepidation, and looking at the paper not knowing where to start or what to do. So, seeing a fail mark looming, I just did what I thought was right and was one of the first to leave the room.

Come the day of the results, we were sat in the room and the maths lecturer started giving the results out. My name was given last. Gloom on my face, but he gave me special mention as I had got a Distinction (others had too, and better) but he said that I had struggled all year, and it just showed what could be done. He then came and shook my hand saying, so just myself could hear, "How the hell did you pull that one off Willis?"

So my college days came to a close with a Technicians Part 2 certificate, which I was told was equivalent to a HNC, except the maths wasn't as exacting.

Training Courses

As soon as I came out of my time I was able to go on training courses, these were held at either the Doncaster Works Training School or the Derby School of Transport and both places were as different as chalk and cheese.

Doncaster courses were held within the main works in several classrooms on the corner of the site near the canteen and paint shop. All the trainees were put in lodgings in the town and expected to get a bus to and from the works and given a bus pass to do this. The first time I went, I ended up sharing a dingy attic room with a Polish fitter from Stratford. He was extremely polite, and after the evening meal each night he would go to the room and sit writing great long letters to his wife which he would post every morning. A few years later all courses were timed so that most people could travel each day, which meant longer days, but everyone was happier that way.

The classrooms were all rigged out with working mock ups of different types of brake systems, automatic warning systems (AWS) and electrical systems, so the courses were hands on as well as the theory. No meals were provided other than a coffee break in the morning or afternoon, so at lunch time we had to go and fend for ourselves, which was usually a pie from a local shop just outside the main gates.

The Derby courses were held in the ex London Midland & Scottish Railway training college for management on London Road. This was a purpose built building with a Principal in charge and a strict protocol in place that must have been carried over from the LMS days. Each student had his own little room with a bed, wardrobe and desk, hardly room to swing a cat in; bathroom facilities were communal at the end of the corridor. As I have said, the LMS rules were still in place and had to be obeyed, dress at all times had to be smart with a tie unless wearing overalls in a classroom.

The first thing on arriving on the Monday morning was to go through the main door to the porter's room, sign in, and then see what room number one was allocated. More importantly was to look at the board hanging next to the main notice board, which had slide in tabs that showed who had been selected to be the Student President, First Aider or Fire Warden for that week. Apart from being on the top table for every evening meal I'm not sure what the Student President did, I think he was there to act as go between in case of any difficulties between them and us. Luckily my name never went into that slot. I was fire warden twice, which meant knowing all the fire exits and position of fire extinguishers. There wasn't a general alarm bell but one in the warden's room so the wardens were expected to run along their corridors and shout "fire" banging on doors and checking everyone had got out. I was also First Aider once despite my protestations that I wasn't qualified. In my week in that room, which was actually bigger than the rest, I dealt with two cuts that needed sticking plasters, dispensed some stomach ache tablets and a few aspirins. The most important thing was that there was a sewing kit which successfully mended my accidentally torn trousers; I did think, was I supposed to sew a finger or other part back on if required!!

Facilities were provided for the students in the form of a sports room that had a snooker table, table tennis and darts, a small bar that was only open for half an hour before dinner and two hours afterwards. In the centre of the building was a large area with comfortable chairs, a large table with a couple of chess sets and several copies of all the national papers and a small television that always seemed to have the news on. The morning and afternoon coffee breaks were held in there, so there was a timetable of which course was in for coffee and at what time.

The school was run under authoritarian rules at all times but it has to be said all the meals were five star. Each person had his own napkin ring with the room number on, which was used at every meal each day, the napkin being renewed each day of course. Another dread was to look at the board by the door as you went into the dining room to see if your name was on it, because if so it meant you were on the top table that night to sit with the Principal, lecturers and any visiting big wig. We all had to remain standing until the Principal had come in, sat down and then the rest of the top table would sit followed by everyone else. The board also had the seating arrangement on it for that night; this was so pupils were sat with different people every night to mix the conversation up so to speak. I never ended up on the top table; in fact I don't think any of the motive power lads ever did, which said something. There were waitresses dressed in proper uniform at each meal, though they only served table at the evening meal. I can remember a starter for dinner which had a trout staring up at me from the plate, I hadn't a clue what to do with it so had to sort of poke around at it and watched what others did, but I think the majority were in the same boat as I was!

Breakfast was a serve yourself buffet, but again the food was excellent quality and you could have as much as you wanted. Lunch was the same arrangement and again one had to be careful not to eat too much or falling asleep in the afternoon in class was a high probability.

The school was now mainly used to teach Signal & Telegraph staff about all the modern things that were being introduced on their side of the railway but us mere shed fitters and electricians had to make do with three prefabricated classrooms away from the main building. But they were well equipped; well how many classrooms have a 1160hp Sulzer diesel engine in them! In an adjoining part was the main part of a class 47 control cubicle and cab controls which controlled the diesel engine and its output to a load bank. This was ideal, as all sorts of faults could be put on by the instructors, either electrical or mechanical depending on the course being run that week. When I did my electrical training there, I was there for two weeks and I met a fitter from Stratford, who, like me, was interested in the electrical side of things and we thought we knew a thing or two already. So when the class was split into pairs we made sure we were together, we also had the same sense of humour.

After a lot of classroom theory on certain classes of loco's, including learning how to read schematics etc. the instructor would send us a pair at a time into the classroom with the aim of starting the diesel and getting power and it was against the clock to fix the faults so that it did. We were the last in and it didn't take long to find the disconnected wire or contacts with nail polish on, and the diesel roared into life and then with power on. But we then shut it down and rapidly put some of our own faults on as the instructor had. So come the next day the instructor tried to start the engine to explain something, with no joy. Eventually he found out why, but then he couldn't get power, and that took him a while to sort out too. Later he said quietly to us both "Clever buggers eh, no one's done that to me before, and by the way, you two were the fastest at finding the faults".

Another classroom had complete brake systems mounted on the walls. This allowed valves to be changed easily and fault finding to be traced very easily as the valves were all next to each other, not like on loco's where they were scattered all over the place. Modern loco's have all the valves, where possible, in the same place on a brake frame.

My first two courses were on brake systems, Westinghouse and Davies and Metcalfe. Whilst both followed basic principles there were very big differences in the way each did the same job. As soon as one learnt that a diaphragm with two different pressures on it could do all sorts of things, brakes became easy. After these courses I became very interested in brake systems which lasted me my entire career and even though only 22 years old I soon became the depot expert, with faults being left for me to sort out if they couldn't be repaired during the previous shift. I also became adept at repairing all sorts of valves, until we were told that depots were only allowed to change complete valves, but if no valves were in stock we still did a repair rather than have a loco stood.

I can remember having an argument with a senior driver at Thornaby about brakes. His argument was the responsibility and the lives he had in his hands in stopping a train which made him important, and I couldn't agree more. He didn't see though that I might repair several brake systems in a week, so I had several trains during that week and longer, that relied on me or others repairing and testing them properly. So we had a lot more lives in our hands all the time, including his, and this responsibility lasted for months, not just the one shift as he did.

To a lesser degree the electrical courses made schematics and electrical systems understandable and I could usually hold my own against the electricians on the depot or at least understand what they were on about, and I could usually find a fault given time.

At Doncaster I did more training on brakes, the EQ vacuum system was an attempt by Gresham & Craven to emulate the self-lapping ability of the air brake. The brake handle in the EQ system controlled the level of vacuum in a reservoir, which through the medium of a relay valve set the amount of vacuum in the train pipe, which self-lapped and it would stay at that setting continually. A duplex gauge showed the EQ reservoir vacuum and also the train pipe vacuum, so the driver could see what he was asking for and what the train pipe was actually at. It had also, for the first time in a vacuum system, allowed a brake application to have either a passenger timed or goods application. It took drivers some time to get used to it and there were problems with valves sticking and filters getting blocked, so there was always some attention required to keep it working properly, plus it came too late in the day as the way forward was now with air brakes.

The AWS system was part of the brakes system on a loco and as soon as one's mind accepted a small lever sat in a small round box suspended under a bogie travelling at a 100mph could be pivoted by a magnet it passed over, then everything was simple. A green signal meant two track magnets would pivot the lever back and forwards which through relays would give the driver a bell, signifying the signal showed clear. A red or yellow signal would only have one track magnet so that the lever pivoted but didn't return, again relays would then give the driver a horn sounding, which, if he didn't push a button, meant the brakes would automatically go on. Well it's a bit more complicated than that but it hopefully gives you an idea of how it works.

So by the early 70s I felt competent to do everything asked of me and the five year apprenticeship and a few years of courses had been worthwhile and stood me in good stead for the years to follow.

Supervisory years start

The Supervisory set up in the late 6os from the bottom up was a grade A and grade B who worked shifts 24/7 and they were under the control of a grade C who worked day shift Monday to Friday.

A year after coming out of my time a vacancy for an 'A' grade Supervisor appeared, which I applied for but didn't get, as a fitter from Darlington DMU depot was given the post. I was disappointed, as I knew Thornaby and all the heavy work that was done there, which anyone from Darlington wouldn't, as they only looked after Diesel Multiple Units, but it was my first try and the interview was experience for the future. A few weeks later, for some reason the new 'A' decided that it wasn't for him and went back to Darlington as a fitter, enter Joe I'anson again. He went to see the Shedmaster and told him that as I had been the only other contender for the job, unless there was a reason for not appointing me then I should be appointed, so a few days later I had a letter in my hand saying I had been appointed 'A' Supervisor at Thornaby. So started my climb up the ladder to eventually becoming Production Manager with EWS. But that's way in the future and not part of this book.

The 'A' Supervisor was really a runabout for the 'B' but had responsibility for the running work side of things, which entailed looking after the staff working in the running roads who dealt with loco's coming in that required refuelling, 'A' exams and minor repairs. Any larger exam required lots of paper work creating and setting out, so that was my job too. Remember, no computers then, all exam cards came from the stationery store and had to be put together with extra sheets as needed.

One of the things both Maintenance and Running Supervisors got used to were drivers that came with the intention of not causing trouble exactly, but wanting everything to be exactly right all the time, whether it be the condition of the loco, the paperwork, the train, the signalling, or whatever they came across.

I'm afraid my memory for names is very poor but the name Mullins springs to mind as being one such driver. He was a perfectly nice chap but if it was known he, or any of the others who tried to emulate him, was coming on duty, the running foreman would have his loco selected and a spare driver go round it to make sure everything was okay, which meant we got a repair book full of trivial repairs. If we could, we would have had a fitter on the loco already, and made sure all the sands worked (which wasn't easy in some cases as wet sand in sandboxes was a problem with all loco's to some degree) wipers, washers, all windows cleaned, you name it we looked at it, then the loco would be left and we'd just wait.

It was extremely rare that one of these drivers would get on the loco and just go, and when I was on duty I'd stand by the door with my hand out waiting for the repair book. To be fair these drivers always walked up with a friendly smile as they handed me the repair book. What you did not do under any circumstances was say or do anything that was critical of them or their behaviour, as they would never leave the depot, it not being unknown for them to get some repairs done and then go and find some more, always trivial.

For some reason, their thinking was that the BR rule book said that a loco had to be, in the driver's (!) opinion, safe and fit for purpose. Other drivers didn't mind, if for example a sand wasn't working or the window washer was faulty or a wiper blade was a bit iffy, but these few wanted everything spot on all the time, every time.

37065 on the Matterson Jacks in 9 road

I continued as an 'A' Supervisor for some years and then there was a change of grading and the A's became B's and likewise the B's C's and over them was a Chief Maintenance Supervisor and that's how it continued until I became Tool van Supervisor 'C'.

Whilst a 'B' Supervisor I seemed to be usually on with Dick Garbutt, a grade 'C', and we got on well. I can remember one New Year's Eve on nights there weren't many staff on, so to pass the time away, the two of us re-blocked a class 37, refitted a set of side rods to a shunting loco, and renewed a buffer on a class 31. Another day Dick was in the straight sheds where the 'Matterson Jacks' were (these would lift a loco body off its bogies) and I happened to walk in. The first thing I saw was that one of the bogies of the loco they were lifting was still fastened to the body by one bogie to body sling which had fallen back into place, and the bogie was already several feet in the air at one corner. The bogie was just on the point of tipping into the pit, with heaven knows what consequences, when I shouted stop!!! Luckily the fitter on the control panel heard me and the lift stopped. Dick was at the far end of the loco and hadn't spotted the problem whilst the fitters had been chatting away and no one was looking at what was happening at the end furthest away from them. Carefully lowering the body and getting a jack to push the bogie square had things sorted, and the lift started again with a bit more care this time.

Steam Locomotive Preservation

The Q6 and J27 (now belonging to the North Eastern Loco Preservation Group) under restoration in the roundhouse at Thornaby in the early 1970s. A group of volunteers pose for the camera. Maurice Burns and Peter Hutchinson crouch around the dome.
JM Boyes / Armstrong Railway Photographic Trust

Whilst a 'B' Supervisor my backshifts were enlivened by the North Eastern Locomotive Preservation Group. NELPG had purchased a class J27 and Q6 on withdrawal from Sunderland depot these were then brought to Thornaby and stored in the roundhouse. On Tuesday nights volunteers would turn up and overhaul these locos. A newly formed group, they had very little experience or tools, so their leading lights, Maurice Burns and Peter Hutchinson, were always in the office wanting to borrow tools or ask questions. I spent many a happy hour on Tuesdays helping with the repairs and overhauls, and being in the sixties there weren't the HSE problems, so I could let them use the crane that was in the roundhouse for lifting chimneys etc.

Eventually came the day when each loco could be steamed and moved. Chris Cubitt, a secondman at Thornaby and NELPG volunteer, arranged to have a driver available so they could be driven out of the roundhouse along the outlet road and back. The two loco's eventually made their way to the North Yorkshire Moors Railway, then still in its early embryonic years.

Their next purchase was the K1 62005. Of course this had to come to Thornaby on its way to the NYMR and was overhauled in the roundhouse. Again I helped in everyway I could and once the overhaul was completed the K1 was painted in LNER green. By that time there weren't many footplate men passed out on driving steam locos and Stan Hindmarch on shed duties was grabbed to do the honours on its first steaming.

Whilst mentioning the NELPG and going forward some years in my writing, Thornaby hosted the J27 on a couple of occasions, once being when it came to have the axleboxes overhauled and re-metalled, all the work and machining being done by a young fitter, Mike Hewitt, and of course the re-metalling by Lenny Sherris. The A2 'Blue Peter' came to Thornaby and was given an overhaul; again I helped where I could with advice and tools etc. Unfortunately 'Blue Peter' had a severe mechanical failure at Durham and was hauled to Thornaby for investigation and eventual repair. This was a long term job as several large components needed major attention. I was by then on the tool vans and wasn't able to assist as much as before.

The NYMR was host to an ex Lampton Colliery 0-6-2 tank loco, number 29 and that came to Thornaby for axlebox repairs. I was, at that time, a 'C' Supervisor in charge of the shift when some volunteers, along with a couple of my staff, started to remove a wheelset on the wheel drops on 7 road. The bolts that fastened the hornstays in place (these stopped the axleboxes dropping out of the frames) were corroded so they had to be burnt off. Despite this being done hundreds and thousands of times over the years since the depot was built, that day proved to be the time that a red hot nut fell down off the drops table and down into the pool of water and oil that always sat in the bottom of the drop hole.

K1 2005 on its first steaming, resplendent in LNER Apple Green. Driver Stan Hindmarch in the cab.

Bill Sharp

TAKING THE WEIGHT

The oil ignited and within seconds the drop hole bottom was a sea of fire with the flames going up and through the frames of No 29 and round the boiler. Some futile attempts were made to put the fire out with extinguishers while I dashed to the office and called for the fire brigade. Coming out of the office and looking at the flames roaring into the air I grabbed a member of my staff and we ran a large hose from a nearby hydrant down the crane drop hole, and he and I stood at the seat of the fire pouring gallons of water onto an oil fire!! I think all the water cooled the fire down to the point where it went out. I climbed up the drop hole ladder feeling pleased with myself to be met by an irate fire officer who played war with me for putting the fire out! Such is life. There were three fire engines stood outside the shed doors, all with nothing to do, so chuntering, they all went home.

After a look around the drops I rang the DOME Supervisor to come out, and after a good application of grease on the screw threads and running the drops up and down a few times, he declared them safe to use. So within an hour of the fire starting everything was back to normal, and work restarted on removing the wheelset. If I remember correctly, my log book entry for the incident took about four lines and no one queried what had happened, an everyday occurrence dealt with and sorted. Luckily, apart from a bit of scorched paintwork around the boiler, No 29 suffered no damage.

Flame proof shunters

In the early seventies BR won a contract to supply shunting loco's to the Shell Refinery at Teesport. For this task Thornaby was allocated three converted 204hp shunters (class 03) D2046 – D2057 – D2093. They had been converted at the 'Hunslet Works' in Leeds, and the conversion meant changing any equipment that may cause a spark during operation, as the refinery was a place where these could cause a major disaster!!!

The first obvious change was that the exhaust had to be cleaned and any sparks eliminated, and this was achieved by fitting a large box to the right side of the loco footplate. The box held an amount of water and on top were mounted four large filter units, each composed of a gunmetal frame that held several hundred stainless steel plates, each 32 thousands of an inch apart. The exhaust was led into the base of the box, which in theory cooled it, then if any sparks got through the water they would be killed when they went through the small gaps between the plates. The other requirements were that all electric lights were in flame proof enclosures, the dynamo was a sealed unit, brake blocks were made of a Ferodo composition, and finally, the starter motor was an air motor. This was fed from a high pressure air cylinder at 450psi via a valve in the cab, the cylinder being continually topped up by a high pressure (HP) compressor. Thus, the loco was intrinsically safe when working in areas within the refinery that may contain inflammable gases.

As with the boilers, what were bought off the shelf as long proven items, soon started to fall to bits or not work for various reasons. We were soon engaged in a battle to keep the loco's running, two being needed in service at any one time and one spare, each shift in the shunting shed having a loco to deal with. The only good job was re-blocking, as the Ferodo brake blocks were a lot lighter than the cast iron ones.

First to go were the HP compressors, the HP valves fell to pieces, because a little three legged fork that pushed the HP valve off its seat once max pressure was reached, lost its legs which ended up in the cylinder and damaged the pistons. Then there were the starter motors which had a disc valve on the main shaft, this soon scored and leaked by so the motor wouldn't run, despite using the special grease which we were assured would stop this happening. HP leaks on the pipe work meant no air to start when required. No leak finding spray in those days.

The biggest problem we had though was with the wash box and filters on the exhaust system. Every time a loco came back it was two fitters onto it, and it was always found that the box had boiled dry, so the loco's went back to Doncaster works one by one and had a top up tank fitted under the roof above the engine, which bled water in and kept the tank to the correct level. It was rare a tank came back empty after that.

Then we removed the red hot spark arrestor filter blocks, emptied and washed out the wash box, refilled the box with a mixture of water and a small amount of 'Exmover' (a chemical in powder form used in the loco washing plant), refitted a cleaned set of filters, and it was ready to go back out.

The filters were a bronze cage with rows of stainless steel plates held 32 thou" apart. Of course the exhaust, even after going through the water in the wash box, still had carbon in it, and this stuck to the plates slowly blocking up the gaps. The original instructions from Hunslet were that soaking in a hot Exmover water solution would loosen the carbon and a water jet would finish the job in an hour. Despite having a tank with a gas jet under it and boiling them, they just got more blocked over time. We then had to resort to stripping all the plates out and cleaning them by hand, finally refitting the plates, which wasn't an easy job at all as the plates were a tight fit in the filter bodies, a very labour intensive job.

D2046 was a bit smoky to start with and the filter packs on this loco soon got choked up leading to back pressure in the exhaust, which meant a sluggish engine and even more smoke, a vicious circle. As the contract came to an end there were no spares and the loco's were worn out, so it was a struggle to keep them going to the end. Eventually, we gave up the struggle with the starting system and resorted to push starting them.

Of course these little loco's were being asked to haul several 100 ton tank wagons and this took its toll on the gearboxes and final drive units. Several gearbox changes had to be done along with other major work to keep them going. Thankfully the refinery output dropped now and again, so only one loco was needed so we could catch up with outstanding maintenance and repairs

I don't think anyone shed any tears when the contract finished and the loco's went into store.

Whilst writing this book I tried to refresh my memory of these loco's by using the web, fount of all knowledge, but apart from a very small comment about a modification to the design by Hunslet, I couldn't find a thing.

Tool van days start!!

My tool van experiences actually started back in 1967, when still an apprentice. Up until then the tool vans to me were a black art that was hidden away in 10 road of the straight shed. In there was a motley collection of old converted carriages, some looking as if they were from George Stephenson's time, with a 25 ton 'Craven' steam crane (now resident in the collection at the York Railway Museum). The crane was kept in light steam at all times and all the equipment in the coaches was checked after use and stowed neatly and ready for whatever the next job would be. It was expected that the tool vans would be off the depot within half an hour of getting a call. The running foreman always had an engine tucked away handy, as well as footplate staff so that this time would be met, otherwise questions would be asked from on high.

What appeared to be a secret society of maintenance staff was formed from volunteers from the locomotive maintenance staff to man the tool vans, and as soon as there was a call the word was passed around and off they would go; those off duty would be summoned by messenger. There was a strict hierarchy of those taken, i.e. seniority. Those with the longest tool van service would be called first, except of course for essential members such as the guard (of which more later on) and the crane driver, and maybe even the cook!! The Chief Maintenance Supervisor, or if a big job the Shedmaster, would be in charge, but later on certain Supervisors were trained and they took week about being on call. Those in the shed not being tool van members used to call the tool van gang all sorts of uncomplimentary names, mainly to do with them getting extra money when called out, plus of course lots of overtime. I, being young and foolish, just went along with this, later appreciating exactly what these men gave up for what was in effect a mere pittance in monetary terms, they actually enjoyed doing it and if they had had their way would have done nothing else.

My first chance to see a tool van gang in action was not Thornaby's but the Darlington gang. This was when a 'Clayton' type 1 D8588 (which was brand new at the time) was driven into the bullring at Thornaby and the turntable hadn't been left lined up correctly. The loco drove onto the turntable and ran along the walkway plates for a short distance, so the loco was now sat with one bogie on the track and the other hanging off the turntable side. The Thornaby tool van Supervisor had a look and thought it would take a long time to jack it up safely on packing and move it back, so Darlington was sent for with their 45 ton steam crane (which we would later inherit). The crane was positioned on a diverging track next to the unhappy loco, and it was just possible to get the jib up under the bull ring

'Clayton' Type 1 D8588 in trouble after missing the turntable.

roof and get a lift on the derailed loco and ease it back onto the track. All the under gear had been badly damaged by the dive so the 'Clayton' had to be made safe to haul back to the main works for repair, even though only a few weeks old.

One glorious hot summer day in 1967 the tool vans were called to a derailment, and for some strange reason they were short of staff, so I was volunteered (told) to go along to help (!) and learn something. There were two bogie bolsters off at the entrance to the Malleable Steel Works (Stockton) at the end of the short branch line (the Beck branch) which ran from North Shore to the Malleable works.

Climbing onto the tool vans for the first time was a culture shock as one entered a strange new world; the riding van was an old Gresley brake coach that had been converted into what in effect could be called a snug. The first part was a locker room with a few sinks and a toilet, then next a long compartment formed from several compartments knocked into one and running the length of half the coach with long bench seats and a long table between them, and with old coach cushions scattered about. Each person had his place in the seating arrangement and there was trouble if anyone sat where they shouldn't!! To heat this large space was a guard van stove at one end of the table with a supply of coal. This stove when lit threw out a lot of heat and when the train was moving and a draft was on, the chimney would actually glow bright red from the bottom to the top. The next compartment was a kitchen with a coal fired stove, and the last compartment was the Supervisor's with a small bench seat and a table, chair and a few lockers, (an overhead long locker was taken and used in the next coach we had, and this now resides in my workshop) plus of course another guards van stove. This compartment was slightly upmarket in appearance and quality of fittings from the rest of the coach, as senior officers would use it as a base if at a major derailment.

A Sulzer type 2 was used to haul us out to the derailment, and once there, Jimmy Green the Supervisor got out, weighed the job up and had the staff scurrying around. It wasn't possible to get the crane onto the job, so this meant getting the MFD (Maschinenfabrik Deutschland) jacking gear out. This wasn't the modern lightweight aluminium alloy gear used now, but jacks made from cast iron, beams made from steel girders and a diesel driven water pump with water tank mounted on a huge trolley. Everything weighed at least a ton, and several men with special lifting poles were needed to get the gear out and in position. A special hand powered crane was mounted at the rear of the MFD van to at least get the stuff onto the ground. I just stood and stared at this performance until shouted at to get a move on; it seemed to me to be farcical. When we started to use these jacks it soon turned into a real farce as the pipes to the jacks, the jacks and pump themselves, leaked water at every connection in true fountain style, so we were soon soaking wet, and two men did nothing else but keep the pump's water tank topped up from a huge tank kept in the jacking gear coach. But the gear worked, albeit slowly, and within half an hour the wagons were re-railed, and then came the even harder task of getting everything put away.

A few days later my services were required again. Several 21 ton coal hopper wagons were off at Haverton Hill curve, the other end of the Beck branch. This time the crane could be used and what a difference. Each man knew what they had to do and even though in a tangle, the wagons were back on the track with no effort from the staff other than setting and packing the crane. Being a nice sunny day it was a pleasure to be out there, but I still hadn't got an urge to have anything to do with the tool vans.

Six months before coming out of my time I was told that as part of my further training, if the tool vans were called out during the day, then I should go out with them. I wasn't keen, but I had been told. The other part of the conversation was that I should make every effort to get back to the shed for my normal finishing time. That turned out to be impossible, which they must have known. By now it had been decided to employ a full time Breakdown Supervisor and Jimmy Dean had got the job. He had been a Supervisor in Darlington works in the diesel shops and had transferred to Thornaby when Darlington Works closed in 1965. Also, a year prior to Darlington Steam shed closing, the 45 ton steam crane based there was transferred to Thornaby to replace the venerable 25 ton crane. So I was soon going out several times a week, and a few times I was late getting back so incurred overtime payments which boosted my low pay very slightly. It was obvious that the Maintenance Supervisor wasn't happy about this but there was no way of stopping it happening. All of the jobs tended to be simple one wagon derailments in the yards and the crane was usually used as a quick fix, but if a loco was involved then jacks had to be used as the crane wasn't rated to pick up their weight. Listening to the crane driver though, he said the crane would pick anything up given the chance. (I used this to the full in later years!)

It wasn't until a few weeks had passed that I got a taste of true tool van work. It was a miserable day and pouring down with rain when the call came that a Type 3 was off all wheels at Cemetery North, Hartlepool. We arrived at about three o clock in the afternoon alongside the derailed loco; it had split the points and needed lifting and moving sideways about three feet to get back onto the track. For some reason I couldn't fathom then or now, Jimmy Dean decided to jack the loco up on hand operated hydraulic jacks one end at a time, and then use a jack to push it over in the direction we wanted to go, in effect throwing the loco sideways. In the pouring rain this wasn't an easy or pleasant task and we made slow progress, a few inches gained at a time. At about 20.00hrs an operating Supervisor came rushing up to say that there had been a bad derailment at the entrance to the Wilton branch near Grangetown, which had wiped the small signal cabin out, killing the signalman. So everything was quickly put away and we set off at speed to Wilton. Jimmy Dean wasn't happy about me going there due to the death of the signal man who was still trapped in the remains of his cabin with two wagons on top, so I was dropped off at Thornaby station.

The following day the tool vans returned to Cemetery North to complete the re-railing of the Type 3, again using hand jacks, a slow laborious job, but at least the rain had stopped.

I should explain that in those days the tool van men just kept working. There were no restrictions on the hours that could be worked continually, so a man could start work at 07.00, finish at 16.00 go home for ten minutes, then be called out and work for two days continuous before signing off. There was a rule that said a man had to have 9 hours rest after a tool van call lasting 10 hours or more, but that was loosely upheld to suit the tool van manning and person's needs!!! So in these circumstances there could be a welcome addition to a man's wages.

Supervisor Tool vans

After six months of being seconded to the tool vans I came off and there was no further involvement until early in 1976 when the Breakdown Supervisor of that time, Mick Thomas, indicated that he would be coming off that job. Jimmy Dean, by then the Depot Maintenance Supervisor, asked if I would be interested, so after some thought I said yes. I then started going out again with the tool vans but this time to learn the Supervisor's job. I was introduced to all the rules and regulations that had to be known and adhered to and ended up carrying a large satchel containing all sorts of books and pamphlets. At first it was a case of watching how Mick dealt with situations, and then after a few weeks actually being in charge and telling the men what to do, but none of the jobs were startling or difficult, so my confidence was misplaced. After a few months, Mick was given a Grade 'C' Maintenance Supervisor's job in the shed and I was successful in interview to get the Breakdown Supervisor's job, but I still couldn't go out on my own if the crane was to be used, and either Mick or Jimmy Dean had to be there, as I hadn't enough experience to be let loose or pass an examination to get a certificate for the crane.

The following week came my first derailment on my own, and it had to be what was to me then a big one!! A class 37 was off all wheels at Clay Lane sidings within the steelworks complex at South Bank. Steelworks maintained track wasn't exactly the best, they tended to use steel sleepers with tapered steel keys securing the rails to them, and it used to fall to bits quite easily with the loads put on it by our large loco's, unless well maintained. This is what had happened here, the rails peeling apart as the loco derailed then ploughed its way through them. The day couldn't have been colder or wetter. We arrived on a nearby track, and I got down from the riding van and just stood there and stared at this loco sat in the mud, no usable track under it and the nearest good track twelve feet away. "What on earth do I do with this" I thought, "Have I made a stupid decision saying I'd take this job on?" After a few minutes Dave Lindsay came up and said "So how are we tackling this then?" I just shrugged my shoulders and said nothing as panic set in. "Right we'll get the MFD gear out then shall we?" "Err yes" I replied. So the lads set to and we had the loco lifted up on four jacks on trolleys and beams within an hour. By then I could feel confidence returning as I saw how and what had to be done. So without realising it I regained control of the situation from the team as we pushed the loco sideways along the beams using the jacking system, until it was above good track and then lowered down onto it. This was just as well seeing that Mr George Mitchell, the wagon engineer who was on call for derailments that day, called in just as we were finishing off.

My baptism of fire was over and I always kept an ear open from then on to the old hands for a few years after that, because they knew more than I did. As time passed I also realised that on this job you never stopped learning, as even the simple jobs were unique and each needed a different solution. As the weeks passed I dealt with lots of derailments, sometimes using the crane, jacks, re-railing ramps, or just a good old pull it back the way it had come, though the P'way department wasn't happy about us using this method. I had a little blue book produced by British Railways that was a sort of best practice rule book for Tool van Supervisors. This explained the basics of each method of re-railing. In it, the last few immortal words said 'Whatever methods are used for re-railing it should be borne in mind that it is a priority to clear the line safely and as quickly as possible with the least damage, using whatever means necessary'. I certainly put these last words to the test over the coming years!!!

So the months of 1976 passed and a few simple crane jobs came our way so I could get in some practice, and then I was summoned to Newcastle Divisional Headquarters in November to pass my crane test. To say I was a quivering heap when I went into the office of Mr Reeves the Divisional Engineer, would be an understatement. I stood in front of his desk facing both Mr Reeves and his assistant, John Wanless (ex Shedmaster, Thornaby). These two were feared back at the depot, as both of them were renowned for coming to the depot unannounced and finding all sorts wrong, letting one know in no uncertain terms. As an example, if Mr Reeves was known to be coming, everyone had to rush round to make sure there were no tail lights or cab lights left switched on, or loco's not chocked, as Mr Reeves would spot them from a mile away and speak sternly to the Supervisor, but this particular day they couldn't have been nicer. I was quizzed on aspects of tool van work, rules and regulations, and finally detailed questions about the crane and how it should be used, or more specifically how it shouldn't be used. I walked out of the office an hour later clutching a signed certificate saying I was competent to supervise a Cowan and Sheldon 45 ton capacity rail mounted breakdown crane.

A DMU that had collided with a class 31 on the depot in 1986. How one doesn't see another loco on the depot whilst shunting beats me.
Dick Watson

TAKING THE WEIGHT

Don't do that again

My first brush with railway officialdom came fairly soon after getting my crane certificate when the Hydrocyanic Tank train came off at Ferryhill one evening. This train conveyed hydrocyanic acid in 45 ton tank wagons from ICI Billingham, and was a special train, as this acid was, at that time, one of the most dangerous chemicals transported by rail. In the loco and guards van was a satchel containing two hypodermic syringes, with the instruction 'To be administered immediately by a doctor only'. The instructions for this train said that in the event of a leakage of acid the train crew must be injected at once if they came into contact with any of the gas from the acid, as death would result quickly from the first breath of the gas. Which is fine, but where do you get a doctor from that quickly, especially in the middle of nowhere? The train was also exempt, for obvious reasons from the general rule that a member of the footplate staff or guard would walk back to see what had happened to the train.

Back to the derailment. The train had derailed completely after the track gave way as it approached Ferryhill on the line from Stockton. All the tanks had stayed upright, but as a precaution, all of Ferryhill town had been evacuated. Gateshead Tool vans had been sent for and they were to lift the tanks up and place them on a nearby siding. The rear of the train was composed of 12 ton vans and we were given the task of dealing with all fifteen of them. Coming up wrong line we were able to get alongside them and lift them onto the yard headshunt that ran alongside at that point. Setting the crane up with the two front slides out and the jib runner and relieving bogie still attached, we started the job. We were able to get two vans for each setting of the crane, which helped speed the job up. Just as we were dealing with the last two, along came Jack Wanless, the Newcastle DME at that time, "Very well done Willis" he said, "but the next time I see you keeping a load up in the air for longer than necessary I'll chop your head off" (well actually my head wasn't the word he used...), and off he strode back to the tanks and the Gateshead crane. What I had been doing was lifting the van up to a height to get it over the jib runner and then keeping it at that height whilst the crane slewed around until the van was above the headshunt rails. What I should have done was, as soon as the van was clear of the jib runner, lower the van to just above the rails and then continue slewing round until ready to put it on the rails. If the crane had started to overturn, then being so close to the ground, the van would have touched down and taken the weight off the hook and the crane would have stabilised. My way wouldn't have had that safety margin. Another obvious lesson learnt.

Tool van calls and staffing

I came onto the re-railing scene just before Health and Safety experts (!) and red tape killed off initiative, and also the number of derailments was falling drastically as lines and sidings were closed, old stock and loose coupled freights disappeared, and in effect the causes of derailments were being steadily removed. I remember at the end of 1977 saying to the tool van gang "Well we have had 393 calls this year" (equalling more than one a day) and an old timer said "What? That's poor, I can remember a few years ago when we used to get more than 600 in a year!!" What has to be remembered is that yards and sidings used to have wagons derailed but not call for the tool vans, then when a derailment happened that had to be dealt with they would ask for all the other wagons to be re-railed as well, so in a day the tool vans could tot up 5 plus derailments as each separate wagon counted as one and had to have a report form filled in. Yards could also re-rail wagons themselves by using re-railing ramps and a loco to pull the wagon back on, so we only got the ones they couldn't manage or sometimes made worse, though they were not supposed to re-rail bogie vehicles via this method as the centre pins could be damaged, but that didn't stop them trying.

Being on the tool vans in those days was a vocation, there being hardly ever any changes in the basic gang, a case of dead men's shoes (as also, firemen had to wait for a driver to die before they could move up to be a driver in steam days). When I took over the tool vans some of the staff had been going out with them nearly all their working lives, and me taking over when I was only 29 years old (a mere bairn to them) was a bit much for them to take on board, so there were a few months where I had to assert my authority forcefully. Once I had shown that I was capable of dealing with situations and perhaps more importantly, being a fair person, then they couldn't have been more helpful, or worked any harder when the occasion demanded it. The staffing of the tool vans, as I have said, was by volunteers from the locomotive repair department only, a gang of nine went out every time, no matter how small or big the job was. In those days the gang was mainly formed of fitter's mates, one or two of which were the crane driver and his relief, plus a boilersmith (to do any gas burning and look after the crane boiler, washouts etc.) and a fitter to deal with anything needed to make a locomotive fit to travel. Up until the late sixties there had been no Carriage & Wagon (C&W) staff allowed (!) on the tool vans but by the time I came on the scene, Dave Lindsay, a C&W fitter, had been taken on for some years as part of the gang, and was useful in dealing with, and making wagons fit to move after re-railing. As the years passed by and staff retired or left, it became more difficult to get volunteers, so the ratio of grades was abandoned and any grade was taken to fill a vacancy.

Our area

Another aspect that soon became clear was that territorial rights meant everything to each depot's tool van gang, and of course the Supervisor, Each depot was given an area to cover and woe betide any control that sent the wrong tool vans into someone else's area!! In my time, Thornaby covered from South of Easington Colliery on the Stockton to Newcastle coast line, and Reilly Mill (South of Durham) on the East Coast mainline down to north of Thirsk Station, and all branches and lines between those points. If any depot got wind of an incursion into their area by another gang that they should have attended, then a claim would be straight into the Shed Master for payment to all the gang for the lost call. Usually this worked, and after investigations, payment would duly appear in the pay packet. Rivalry between tool vans was such that it wasn't unknown for a Supervisor, if he knew of another derailment in his area, to tell the operators he wouldn't be long with this derailment, or say I'll go and do that one and come back to this later, depending on which was more important. Another aspect was, if it was a big job he would say we can manage this, no need to bring another tool vans in to help, thus ensuring that they would get more time in doing the job, this depended on how cute to tool vans wiles or forceful the Operating Manager on site was. You can judge for yourselves where I sat in this aspect of tool van work!

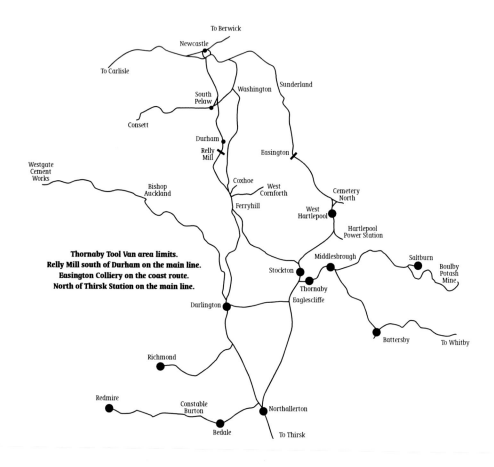

Map of Thornaby tool van area

Find the cause

The first thing a Tool van Supervisor had to do on reaching the derailment and before starting work, was to get all the details and come to a conclusion with the Operating Manager and P'way Supervisor on site as to the cause of the derailment. An agreed cause had to be found and put in our reports. Mainly the cause was very easily found and the majority were either down to the track being faulty, strenuously being denied by the P'way Supervisor of course, or mismanagement of the points or loco by the yard staff, guard or driver. I became expert at deciphering the faint marks left on the railhead or trackwork by wheels as they derailed, which gave the clue as to the cause of the derailment. Of course there were some, especially on plain track on the mainline, which weren't obvious to us, and expert help had to be called in, there being a special department based at the Derby Technical Centre, which had specialist tools to look for voids under the track and other defects on the track or vehicles. In all my time there were only two derailments I attended that could be put down to a fault on the loco, and both of these were due to loose tyres on class 37s at a time when drivers were having trouble making sure that there were no dragging brakes after a brake application when working in multiple. Also derailments due to faults on wagons were not that common, usually being broken springs, sharp flanges or rotationally stiff bogies.

Characters

There were, as to be expected, characters amongst the gang, a few of which I'll mention now. The guard, Eddie McLean, was a fitter's mate. During the wartime years there had been a shortage of guards, so getting one to take the tool vans out had been a problem, therefore it was decided to train up a member of the tool van gang to act as guard. Eddie at that time a young man had been chosen and trained, and since that time had continued to act as guard just for the tool vans. This obviously caused a lot of trouble with the existing guards, who said he wasn't properly trained, didn't have the route knowledge and other arguments about his fitness for the job, but Eddie took refresher exams and never failed, so despite the best efforts of the guards and their union, Eddie stayed, thank goodness, in place as our resident guard. He knew exactly what to do when we arrived at a derailment so that the crane or the jacking van was placed exactly in the right place without me having to say a word. Whenever he was not available we had to have a proper (!) guard but they couldn't do it as well as he did, and sometimes we had to wait hours until one was available. Eddie was the guard en-route and once the tool vans arrived on site he busied himself with helping the cook. It was rare for him to be involved in the heavy work of setting the crane up or jacking.

Eddie was a fount of working railway knowledge and always boasted he could go anywhere, always refusing a conductor guard if one was offered. This was put to the test one day when we had to go over into the wilds of Yorkshire to a colliery, as we were the only available crane at the time. We set off and changed engine crews at York, then at Sheffield, whilst Eddie stayed in charge. Eventually we were stopped at a signal box and told that a conductor guard was coming to take over the train. Eddie went berserk at this and went into the signal box and had a gentle word with the controller. Coming back to the train he told the driver to continue. I asked what had happened, "Oh I just told the controller I knew the road right into the colliery and he has let us go on". I was having my doubts about this the further we went, until we arrived at a small signal box in the middle of nowhere just before the colliery. We stopped at a red flag held by the signal man who said "I've been told your guard doesn't know his way into here", Eddie leaned out of the window and said "Hello there Fred how are you doing?" "Good heavens" he replied "is that you Eddie?" What could I say!? It turned out Eddie had been there several times during the war so knew the signal man, and of course the colliery sidings, so we just went straight in...... I never doubted anymore that Eddie could take us anywhere in the country, which he did.

Spike Humphreys, a fitter's mate, was the cook when I took over, and he was a master at providing hot food at the drop of a hat on the battered old coal stove. He, along with Eddie the guard, seemed to know exactly where every shop and fish and chip shop was, no matter where we were, and would disappear to stock up, but I somehow think pubs were included in that list too. The kettle was always on the boil and I would hate to think how many cups of strong tea we drank, as the cups always seemed to be full and steaming. The food that appeared on the plates was un-nameable and made of strange ingredients, but it always tasted alright and no one was ever ill!! When you're cold and tired you'll eat anything and it always gave you strength to carry on, no matter how many hours you had put in.

Jack (John) Wickham, another fitter's mate, was the resident backend man. The backend man's job was to watch the back wheels of the crane when lifting a load. If the crane started to tip over, then first of all the rail clips loosely fastened to the track would tighten, then if nothing was done to stop the lift, the wheels on the track furthest away from the lift would start to lift off the rail. In theory the rail clips were supposed to lift the track at this point so that when the crane came back down the track was still underneath it, but it never seemed to work that way. So Jack had an important job as the Supervisor was too busy dealing with the lift to wonder what the back of the crane was doing. If Jack thought it had gone too far then he would blow his whistle once and the crane driver would stop the lift. If he thought it serious enough Jack would also shout "drop it" but that was a dangerous thing to do in itself as staff may be near the load and be injured if the crane driver decided to drop the load.

An explanation of setting the crane is needed at this point for those unfamiliar with railway cranes:-

The cranes I had the pleasure of using were all built by Cowan and Sheldon of Carlisle, being 45 ton capacity steam cranes, and a rebuilt 75 ton ex-steam crane that now had an American 2 stroke diesel engine driving a swashplate hydraulic pump which, via a control handle, in turn drove two hydraulic motors mounted on the input shaft which originally the steam cylinders had driven onto. There were no mod cons that one sees on the later telescopic jib rail cranes or even the oldest road cranes. Apart from the jib, lifting, slewing and rail travel motions, everything was done by hard graft. The slides were cranked out by a hand ratchet, as was the pulling down onto the packing by a screw, initially using a hand ratchet and finally a long steel bar with several blokes swinging on the end to achieve the necessary force. No moving a small handle and watching a hydraulic jack do the work. We were tough in those days, doing that no matter the weather or conditions. Weight relieving bogies were used to spread the total weight of the crane over more axles to keep the axle loading down, thus there was a small bogie at each end with two axles each. Via a bell crank mechanism which coupled into the crane buffer beam, it was possible to jack the crank so that the bogie lifted the crane slightly and as their name says, relieved some of the weight off the crane from its own axles. Once jacked to the correct height a pin was locked in place into the crank and the jack released.

Railway cranes are capable of lifting in a 'free on rail condition'; this means there are no slides employed. The axle spring stops would be wound down to a ¼" above each axle spring, the weight relieving bogies lowered, and the rail clips fastened to the rail with a bit of slack so if the crane becomes unstable then they can be seen to be tightening. In this condition the max load that can be lifted with a 360 degree slew is very low, depending on the crane, usually being around the 12 ton mark. The crane can also move along the track with a load within its range. As long as the load is kept within 30 degrees of the track centre line a 76 tonnes Cowan & Sheldon crane can lift its max rated load of 76 tonnes free on rail, with only the corner jacks being screwed down.

Whenever lifting a heavy load, once the relieving bogies have been released, the four slides of the crane are extended, a large area of hardwood packing placed under the end, and the screw of the slide screwed down tight onto a special plate onto the wood packing. This made the crane stable up to its full rated capacity, assuming the ground conditions were good enough. In the case of the 45 ton crane, on the side we would be lifting over, we used two 4' long by 1' wide timbers that were 4" thick (a long four) placed side by side to form the bottom base, then built up from the centre of these with timber 2' x 1' and 6" thick (a six), finally finishing off with similar timber of varying thickness (i.e. 4s, 3s, 2s,and 1s) interlocked to achieve a height close to the slide screw (called double packing). This saved a lot of winding on the screw. If a max lift was needed at right angles to the chassis, then an extra long four would be put inboard of the screw packing, and hard wood packing built up under the slide, and finally wedges driven in to give a bit more area onto the ground. The 76 tonnes crane used the same method but the base timbers were a hefty 6 foot long and 6 inches thick, (a long six) those took some carrying!! If a slide was needed for a light lift then a single long four would be used with a single pillar of 6s etc. (single packing).

Once I had got experience of heavy lifts I decided that, rather than watch staff flogging themselves by riving the slide screws down with a long bar to put enough pressure on the packing to support the crane, it would be better to use the inboard base packing to put a 50 ton hydraulic jack on and literally tip the crane backwards, then pack the slide end tight, screw down and then release the jack. The weight of the crane then pushed the packing down solidly without the staff wearing themselves out, the inboard packing then being wedged tight. Using this method it was very rare that one had to take a heavy lift, put it back down, and tighten the packing before lifting again.

Towards the end of my tool van career I had my two yearly re-examination on the 76 tonne crane, and there were some old wagons that needed lifting away from the track, which meant taking the crane to its limit regarding radius. The ground was soft so I had the staff put inboard packing on the slides, (which the instructor hadn't seen done before), and then jack the crane backwards and pack the slides tight. The instructor stopped me doing this and asked what on earth I was doing. I explained, so he let me continue. Once set, we lifted the wagons right out as far as the radius of the jib would allow and the crane didn't move at all. This impressed the instructor, who said he couldn't use it as an official method, but he would pass the tip onto any who hadn't been using the idea before, as it saved time and effort.

The official instructions for the cranes always said that the weight relieving bogies should be removed from the crane before doing any (!) lifting whatsoever, but I never saw that done whilst I went out in the years before taking over. If undertaking a light lift then they weren't even released. On a heavy lift they would be dropped down once the slides were packed tight, but not uncoupled. If they were going to be in the way then they would be removed, and either pushed further down the line or lifted out of the way. When they had to be replaced, then it became obvious why they were never removed unless necessary!! As they could take some getting back into place and the crank re-located, sometimes the bogies had to be pushed quite fast and banged into place, or instead the crane pushed up on wedges to lift it slightly. We have even had to push the crane up and down the track until either a dip or rise in the track achieved the same result. Obviously, when the cranes were new and everything spot on, then the bogies just slipped in and out, but once wear set in and spring heights changed, and of course the state of the track, then alignment of the crank was more difficult to achieve.

Again, the official instruction stated that all slides must be used if not working free on rail, and again it was obvious, before I became a Supervisor, that this wasn't adhered to. The Supervisor stated which he wanted out, depending on what was being lifted. So if lifting towards one end, then only the two slides at the end would be used, or if a light lift with no danger of the sudden release of load which would cause the jib to flick back over, then only one would be used. So when I took charge, after a while I had the confidence to use the minimum slides to achieve a safe result, but anything over a 30 ton lift meant all four being out, and if lifting 40 tons plus, then inboard packing as well.

But back to Jack Wickham, (just plain Wick to the regulars on the tool vans) and being the regular backend man. One day we were lifting derailed loaded 21 ton hopper wagons at the max radius for the weight, and I was close to where the wagon was, controlling the crane with hand signals. I happened to look back at the crane and thought it looked odd, so I stopped the lift. Walking back to the crane it was obvious that she was leaning over quite a bit. Walking around to the other side there's Wick sat on a piece of packing, fag in hand and staring at the wheels. "What's going on?" I asked," Nothing" said Wick "she's just getting near the limit". "Which particular limit is that?" I asked. "Well when the wheels are 6 inches off the rail I'll stop the lift" he calmly said. So I looked more carefully at the wheels and there they were about 5" above the rail, plus the screws in the back slides were out of their plates by 8" and waving up and down slightly as the crane hovered in balance. So after getting the crane driver to lower the load and put the crane wheels back on the rail I had a short discussion with Wick. He had been using his 6" above the rail for a lot of years since a Supervisor had told him that's what he wanted, and no one until now had ever queried it!! So after a bit more talk I agreed that I would be happy with hovering an inch above the rail as long as I knew, but no more. Whilst the load was off the hook I had the slides repacked and pulled down and we continued re-railing the wagons. Nothing more was said, but Wick's whistle was used a lot more from that day on!

Ooops didn't see you, another collision on the depot. 5th July 1984. Easiest way was to drive the class 37 back the way it had come (lots of grinding noises) and then jack the class 47 back on.
Dick Watson

When I took over, the crane driver, Albert Hicks, had only a few months left before he retired, and he had been crane driving for years. He knew his (and I mean his) crane inside out and spent a lot of time looking after it, so that as well as being mechanically perfect, it literally gleamed like a new car. It was his baby and he treated it as such. He was also a fanatic about going on every derailment and he never missed a call unless on holiday. Well nearly. One day he had finished work and had gone home to take his family on holiday to the Isle of Wight. A few hours later we got a call for a big derailment at Hartlepool and by the time I had got to the shed from home there was Albert on the crane making sure everything was okay, and a big fire roaring away in the firebox. "What are you doing here?" I asked. "You're supposed to be going on holiday". "Well it's a big job and I'd better be there" he said. So along he came. I never found out how he found out about the call, but his experience came in handy. He had set the family off on the train to the Isle of Wight, promising he would follow them, and then rushed to the shed. I presume his wife was very used to Albert, as it wasn't until two days later that we returned to the shed and Albert set off to catch them up.

Following on from Albert when he retired, Eddie Pearson, a fitter, took the job over, so the old rules of which grade of staff did what were slowly being eroded even then. Eddie was a steady person who did things slowly and deliberately and was seemingly unflappable, (a good trait in a crane driver), and always impeccably dressed with shirt and tie. Well, that is until we went to West Hartlepool to re-rail some wagons in the Old Wood Yard. The Old Wood Yard was a large concentration of sidings that had been put in by the North Eastern Railway in the early twenties to cater for the loading and storage of wagons carrying pit props to the pits. All the sidings were severely curved and looked as if they hadn't had any attention since the track had been laid years ago. In this maze of sidings was an empty wagon, de-railed all wheels. "It's only an empty wagon weighing 8 tons but having the crane with us we'll use it free on rail" I thought. How simple things can soon go wrong!! The crane was set and the location of the wagon meant the jib was nearly at 90 degrees to the chassis, the worst scenario for free on rail, but it was only 8 tons of wagon and well within the crane's 12 ton capacity on the duty chart. The wire ropes were fastened to the wagon with 'S' hooks and lifted. When the wheels were clear of the rails, I asked Eddie to slew right. Slewing right, the wagon came across the rail tops, and for some reason, one of the wheels caught the rail top a glancing blow and the wagon bounced ever so slightly on the ropes. The sleepers under the crane decided now was the time to give way and sagged. Straight away the crane started to tilt over with a rocking motion (called pecking because the end of the jib goes up and down like a bird pecking at seed). All this happened in slow motion and I screamed at Eddie to drop the wagon, but in his panic he opened the regulator and continued slewing, which made the situation even worse, and the crane started to slowly keel over. Eventually he realised what he had done and what I wanted, and let the brake off and the wagon dropped to the floor and the crane recovered and righted itself. Eddie staggered out of the cab and jumped onto the ground, his normal calm demeanour all gone, red in the face, hair and tie askew, moustache drooping, he looked a picture, so I said "Right back into the van, get a cup of tea and we'll start again later". Half an hour later we got back to the job,

Eddie had composed himself, tie straightened and looking as if nothing had happened. We put one slide out and quickly re-railed the errant wagon, crane put away and back to the shed. A lesson well learnt - never use a crane free on rail on dodgy track or severely curved track. (These were the days before near misses were recorded as if events had happened).

Road creeps In

In the early 1980's we had been given an ancient lorry and a half set of MFD jacks, with a small diesel pump set to operate them. I was expected to use this whenever possible for small jobs that the lorry could get close to, thus saving a loco and crew, which would have been required to take the full set of vans. The lorry was a 7½ ton vehicle and could be driven on an ordinary driving licence, though a BR test had to be taken and a certificate issued before it could be driven. Myself and a few of the tool van crew were trained and passed out to drive our new addition, and we used it whenever we could, which wasn't often as most derailments were not accessible by it. The lorry was an ex P'way vehicle and the back half was part crew accommodation and part loading space. It was a work of art having the jacking gear loaded along with sufficient packing and all the other odds and ends, plus a lightweight P'way trolley. Just after getting the lorry, one job we went to was at Middlesbrough Goods Yard which had a weigh bridge, so we asked could we weigh our lorry. Getting the lorry positioned, the operator did his stuff and produced a ticket that showed the lorry was half a ton overweight "And don't forget it will weigh even more when your crew get back in" the operator said!!! So panic stations when we got back to the depot, deciding what we could remove to lower the weight.

Lorries on rails?

In 1982 I was asked to go to Peterborough to collect a 'Unimog'. This had been fitted with small rail wheels that could be lowered so that the 'Unimog' could sit on the track and use its road wheels to accelerate and brake, while the rail wheels guided it along the track. A safety feature was that the rail wheels were loaded hydraulically and kept at a constant pressure automatically. It was spending two months at a time at selected depots for evaluation, and it was now our chance to have ago. It was left hand drive and had another few oddities, so it was decided that two of us needed a quick training course at Peterborough, then be passed out at the same time with, of course, another endorsement on the BR driving certificate and Dave Lindsay was chosen. Taking the train to Peterborough, we had a 5 mile walk to the BR road vehicle depot, where the Unimog and an inspector were waiting. After a brief look around and familiarisation, we took turns in driving for a couple of miles around Peterborough while the inspector assessed us on our driving skills, then after signing our certificates, it was ours.

Having never driven a left hand drive before, it was very strange driving this lump of a machine along the A1 heading to Thornaby, but I slowly got used to it. I had a bit of a panic approaching a roundabout as the steering wheel suddenly didn't want to steer and Dave realised the engine had stopped, so no power steering. The stop handle had managed to work itself partly on, and though the engine would run at speed it wouldn't idle. Pulling into a layby to change drivers, we stopped next to a roadside café van which was burnt out and gently smouldering. The lady owner came over to us and mournfully said, "Eeeh love you're too late its burnt out". As the Unimog was bright red, she thought it was a fire engine!!!!

The Red Unimog on the rails   Dick Watson

TAKING THE WEIGHT

The Unimog was an extremely tough durable machine, but its drawback was that to stay under 7½ ton the storage space was too small for all the jacks we would like to carry, plus the platforms used to get the jacks in and out were too high, so we used it in conjunction with the lorry nearly every time. To get it onto the track, all we did was drive it across the track (which it did quite happily) so that a turntable underneath in the middle lined up with the track. This was then lowered until it picked the Unimog up. The turntable allowed us to rotate the Unimog by hand until the wheels aligned with the track, on lowering it was on the track in no time. Another advantage was, it had an inbuilt pump to work the MFD jacks.

We used the Unimog a lot while it was at Thornaby and it gave us no trouble at all, even though it had to clamber over all sorts of rough ground and track. Using its drawbar we even pulled a loaded 100T oil tanker up a gradient after re-railing it. When we lost that Unimog we then received a yellow one with a different body design, still without enough storage room. This had a different rail guidance system and turntable which weren't as good as the red one by a long way, and we often had to resort to finding somewhere we could drive in line with the track to drop the rail wheels.

Several months after we lost the yellow Unimog I had a visit from Ken Mosely, a design engineer from the BR division of the Plant & Machinery Department. He brought a huge questionnaire to fill in about the two Unimogs' performance and problems in using them. This took several hours to fill in, plus he wanted my views on all sorts of aspects for a future vehicle. A few months more passed and Ken rang again asking if I would take part in a review group on road rail vehicles at a two day seminar at the Derby School of Transport (bringing back memories!). This was interesting as there were other Tool van Supervisors from around the country there, and it was amazing the number of different viewpoints, sometimes conflicting, that came up.

Six months down the line Ken was in touch again, asking if I would go to Worcester to see the prototype vehicle, and of course I snapped his hand off. Meeting up with Ken and the Tool van Supervisor from Stratford (another Bob) at Worcester Station, we waited at the station entrance and in rolled the prototype to take us to the factory.

The prototype 'Bruff' at Toton. Note the side access roller shutter door which was changed to an end door on the production vehicles.

The firm that had the contract to build these vehicles was called 'Bruff' and when the vehicles eventually appeared they were all called 'Bruffs'!! A telephone call for a derailment would always say "We need the 'Bruff'", so the name stuck with them for their whole life, and has been passed onto some newer vehicles since, and even if it's only a lorry or van that goes out, it's still "Send for the 'Bruff'". After some introductions we all climbed into the crew compartment and were treated to a run to the factory whilst the 'Bruff' engineers explained about their new creation.

Based on a Bedford 7½ ton lorry chassis, this was a much bigger vehicle than the Unimog, with a crew compartment and a storage area at the back. To get the wheels in line with the track the wheels were put on extended hubs (which proved their undoing as they got older as the off centre loading caused cracks in the axles). A substantial turntable and rail guidance system were fitted, and on the front were connections for the MFD jacks, compressed air, and 110 volts sockets. On the cab roof a floodlight was fitted that could be raised to light the whole area around the 'Bruff', a safety feature being that when lifted it only went up to a safe height to work under overhead lines (de-energised!!), and an override to go up to it's max height. On this prototype 'Bruff' the storage was accessed by roller shutter doors and a drop down ledge to stand on as the red Unimog had. The crew cab seated six, plus driver, and there were many other features that would help store specific tools or jacks. At the factory we could discuss what we thought about aspects of the design, and hopefully these could be sorted before release.

The official unveiling (to which I was invited) took place at Derby School, with a load of bigwigs peering at it, but it couldn't be put through its paces there, so the following day we were all bussed to Toton Depot's training site where it was put on and off the track several times, and the MFD jacks used, along with airbags. I had reservations about the side access, and thankfully the bigwigs said the same. But overall it was considered a success and another twenty nine were ordered, but with alterations, the main one being access at the back to the jacks etc.,

Our 'Bruff' duly arrived and proved very useful in attending derailments by road, though, as with the 'Unimogs', we used the lorry as well to carry the extra equipment we needed. By this time the old lorry had been replaced with a more modern version thank goodness. Of course one of the first jobs was to affix a Thornaby Kingfisher to both sides.

Thornabys 'Bruff' at Eastgate 14th June 1989. re-railing several cement wagons
Dick Watson

Having the 'Bruff' meant we were now expected to use it whenever possible instead of the rail vans. The operators were told to order the 'Bruff' every time unless it was absolutely obvious the rail vans or a crane were required. So one night, when we were ordered to attend to four derailed Spanish ferry vans on the up slow south of Thirsk, I presumed that the crane would be ordered, but no, the ops manager asked for the 'Bruff' so he could keep the up fast line open.

We drove to Tollerton where there were a few sidings we could use to put the 'Bruff' on the railway easily, and also keep the lorry there. While the lads put the 'Bruff' on the track and put extra packing etc into the 'Bruff' I went up to the signalbox to sign the register to take possession of the up slow. We had to use the signals, so I drove, and once on the up slow and with permission from the signalman, we set off going the wrong way along the line. Being several miles from the derailment I got the 'Bruff' up to 40mph, a rare chance indeed, as usually we only drove a short distance on rail, and being long welded rail we just glided along. It felt very odd driving what was really a road lorry and not steering (the steering wheel was clamped in the straight ahead position) just using the accelerator and brake pedals.

Spotting a red light in the distance we slowed down and then stopped by the op's Supervisor, who then walked us up to the derailment. The ferry wagons were derailed all wheels but upright so it didn't take long to jack the first one up and re-rail it. Our hoses wouldn't reach the next one, so while the lads set the jacks up on that I took the first wagon back to Tollerton hauled by the 'Bruff', another first for us, hauling a wagon some distance, which was fine until I wanted to slow down for Tollerton. It was immediately obvious that a 'Bruff' didn't stop as easily on rail as it did in hauling, as the wheels just picked up and slid and we skidded along, next stop York!! Luckily, dabbing the brakes managed to stop us just past the points to back into the sidings.

Once back on site we had to lift the wagon quite high and pull the track together underneath it, and this was when a dangerous problem arose. The up fast was still open and trains were being stopped at the signal before the derailment site and told to pass at caution. We had only had one train pass up to now, one of our class 37s on a steel train which, though accelerating, only passed slowly. While we had the wagon in the air we were told a passenger train was passing, so we lowered the wagon as much as we could, stood back and waited. This one was a HST and accelerating from a standing start at the signal it flew past us, causing the wagon to sway alarmingly and cause me near heart failure. I checked what was being said to drivers at the signal, and found that the signalman wasn't telling them to pass the derailment site at caution. So I insisted a man was stationed at the signal to instruct the drivers to crawl past us. After that the job was just routine, but a lesson learnt, always check what's being said to anyone working around you.

What environmental issues?

Things in the early eighties weren't as strict environmentally as they are now. A class 37 had smashed through a buffer stop on the headshunt for Ferryhill yard and derailed one bogie. Having obtained permission to stand the tool vans on the up goods line, our loco went into the yard, onto the derailed loco and coupled onto it. Next we jacked the derailed end up and put some old sleepers that were nearby, thank goodness, plus some bits of rail, also just to hand, and laid them on their sides to form a crude railway to support and guide the wheels to the original track end. When we dragged the loco back onto the track we found we had a big problem, as a piece of rail had punctured the fuel tank from end to end and all the fuel had gone into the stream nearby. I informed the ops manager straight away and he rang the local council, but they didn't even bother to send anyone to look at it or deal with it!! Once the loco was pulled back away from the stream we tried to get the piece of rail out of the tank, but despite being a rattling fit in the tank it wouldn't pull out, so attaching a chain to it and using a 3 ton Pul–Lift fastened to the track, we slowly hauled it out a few feet at a time then burnt that piece off to give us room to pull some more out then burnt that bit off too. Once the rail was removed from the tank we hauled the loco up to the yard, checked it over and found hardly any damage to stop it being hauled back to the depot for repairs. Our loco then collected the tool vans and put the dead loco between our loco and the train and we waited for the signal to depart for Thornaby.

Leaving the yard I fully expected to go down the branch at a slow speed to Stillington and then to Stockton, but for some reason we were put onto the mainline to Darlington and our driver, knowing there was bound to be something travelling fast behind us, set off with gusto and soon had us running at our max speed of 45mph. After ten minutes or so I could smell diesel fuel and there was a fine mist of fuel building up on the window of my compartment. I stuck my head out of the window just as the train braked and a great burst of smoke came from the dead loco's bogies. I dived for the emergency brake valve, brought the train to a halt, then walked up to see what was happening and met the secondman coming the other way. Looking at the loco the trailing bogie was lathered in fuel and putting the brakes on had caused this to heat up and smoke. The small amount of fuel left in the tank was slopping around, coming through the two holes and atomising as it hit the track, then covering the bogies and coaches. Knowing we were on the mainline, quick decision time once again, so I isolated that bogie's brakes and told the driver so he could compensate for this, and off we went again. I had to accept we would be putting fuel on the track but given our speed it would be a very small amount in one place. I could see the windows slowly getting covered in fuel but we got back to the depot without further incident. I expected to get a letter about the train stopping on the mainline but nothing appeared, so the signalman hadn't noticed the amount of time it took us to get to Darlington, thank goodness.

Now I had the complete tool vans and crane covered in fuel oil from top to tail, so I had a word with the running foreman and he gave me a spare set of men and loco to haul the complete train, plus crane, through the washing plant a few times. At last the tool vans sparkled like a new pin!!!

Bridging Jobs

In those early years of my tool van career, bridging jobs happened about two or three times a year and were looked on by the gang as easy money earners. Of course, in the old days they had had at least one a month. All railway bridges were replaced, either because they were life expired, needed updating to a more modern design for extra weight carrying or speed increases of either rail or road traffic, or put in for a new road going under or over the railway. In 99% of the cases rail cranes were used either alone, or one at each end of the lift, the emphasis being in those days to do everything in house and not use outside contractors if at all possible. The usual format was a phone call from the office that dealt with tool vans and crane availability to say the crane was required on such and such a date

East Cowton Bridging job with all the gang
L-R Dave Lindsay, Dick Watson, Jack Baldwin, Yours truly, Dave Crossley, Jack Wickham,
Bill Flower, George Singh, John Young (big John) Joe Glass, Ewan Carmichael (secondman)
Dick Watson

and for me to attend a site meeting on a given date. At the meeting the Civil Engineers would be sorting out what they had to do, when, how, time scales etc., including me when any lifting was being discussed.

B6271 road bridge - Northallerton

My first bridging job happened shortly after getting my competency certificate for the crane, and I must admit to being worried, as I had never seen any bridge work being done. The bridge was on the B6271 very near to what was then the Yorkshire Trailer factory at Northallerton. The original bridge was narrow and brick built, and the intention was to replace it with a much stronger, wider and higher bridge (in case electrification of the railway ever took place), made from two large girders and steel cross members. The meeting explained to me that the two main girders would arrive by rail and the crane would be used to lift them into place using a purpose built lifting beam. Once that was done the crane would be used to place cross members so that a road crane either side could lift them into place. A red cross on a sleeper would mark the place on the track where the centre line of the crane would have to be exactly for each lift, as the crane would be on its maximum lift of 45 tons for each main girder.

We arrived on site at 22.00hrs on the Saturday night and what the site meeting hadn't discussed was the weather. It was raining hard and blowing a gale. The brick bridge had been demolished the previous weekend and new supports cast in place during the week. We first of all had to unload the cross members from wagons and then set up for the first big lift, which, being mid summer, was luckily going to be in the early morning light. The main girders were being carried on special wagons and once the crane was set up on its own, (the relieving bogies, jib runner and train having been left well clear of the work site), the lifting beam was attached to the crane hook, the first main girder pushed down next to the crane, and the lifting beam fastened onto the first girder.

Lifting the first main girder into place at Northallerton

TAKING THE WEIGHT

The crane was on solid good ground in the middle of the four track main line, so I had no qualms about the packing settling, and the first girder was soon on its way up into the air. All this had taken place in what was a shallow cutting, and as soon as that huge girder was lifted into the air the wind caught it, and despite having ropes with a lot of men pulling on them, the girder just merrily rotated around until it hit the side of the crane jib. The engineer in charge went blue in the face trying to get his men to pull the girder into the right position, but the wind thought otherwise, so I eventually relented and got my 8 men, who were standing laughing, to pull on the ropes as well. The girder slowly came back into line and we kept on lifting until it was high enough to clear the bearings the girder would sit onto. Once again the wind thought otherwise and it took a long time with the girder floating just above the bearings before the engineer was happy for it to be dropped down in place.

I found out on that job that civil engineers, when building these bridges, worked to at least ½ a millimetre if not less, which I thought quite funny when there is 40 tons of large steel girder swinging around in a gale pulling about thirty men around with it as if they were ants. The crane was then set back under its own steam to a marked position to lift the second girder. This was a repeat of the previous exercise, but this time it was imperative that this girder did not, under any circumstances, touch the first one, as that was just sat waving in the wind and purely resting on its bearings and not fastened down. As before, as soon as we lifted, the wind spun the girder around, but the engineer had been phoning around and had got some extra bodies from other work sites to hang on to more ropes to help with this part of the job, so the girder was soon behaving itself, and whilst not easy or quick, was eventually sat on its bearings. Then we lifted the cross members to the road cranes and the first one was quickly bolted into position, thus making the girders safe and secure at last. Our part of the job was soon over and we could put the crane away, re-marshal the train back together and leave for the shed, so we had only got just under 24 hours in but a welcome addition to the pay packet nevertheless.

No straight Lines, Ketton viaduct near Beaumont Hill, Darlington

25th July 1981

North of Darlington, near Beaumont Hill, the railway passes over some low lying land with the River Skerne winding its way through, so this meant building a low viaduct of several arches to carry the tracks. I was asked to go to a site meeting there to discuss fitting the viaduct with an overhanging concrete parapet so that anyone working on the viaduct had a safe place to get to if a train came along. The job would entail picking concrete beams weighing 20 tons, one at a time, out of a wagon and placing them on the viaduct wall edge, which would be prepared and drilled ready, the beams being bolted and glued into place. I had to have written approval from the civil engineer, as cranes could only be used on bridges, viaducts etc with his written permission, plus it was the middle of summer with plenty of daylight, so no problems envisaged there. Wrong!!

Arriving at 20.00hrs we stopped at the north end of the viaduct, lifted the jib, attached the lifting beam to the hook, uncoupled the relieving bogie and set back to the south end of the viaduct with just the crane. We picked the first of the beams up and set it just above where it was to sit, (the engineers had allowed 45 minutes per beam so that the mainline could be handed back for traffic at 05.00 Monday). Once they had checked everything and placed the glue we lowered the beam into place so the bolts could be put in and tightened. As I have said previously, the civils look for near perfection lining things up and this is what they wanted, especially as this was an end one which the others would line up from, so a bit of fiddling and it was down and fastened. Then the other side beam was dealt with in similar fashion. We were a few minutes longer than expected but close to target time. Moving the crane down, we picked the next beam up and again swung it into place and lowered it onto the wall. Two hours later we were still there, the beam just wouldn't line up with the viaduct or the first beam. The engineer in charge was going frantic at this point as it became apparent the viaduct sides weren't true. Eventually he snapped, and the beam was put down in an average setting. Of course the next one on the other side was just the same and was soon put down, even if out of line. So we carried on in similar vein, beam by beam, each one being out of line by a different amount to the others, but it was taking longer than allowed for every one of them.

When we had placed half of them, disaster struck in the form of the Chief Civil Engineer for the Newcastle Area. He was a formidable character who struck fear into the hearts of the civil engineers in his employ, and was renowned for turning up at worksites at any time of the day or night, checking up on things and letting them know in no uncertain terms if he wasn't satisfied with the work being done. When he arrived and looked along the line of concrete beams wavering along the viaduct wall tops, his face went purple with anger and he exploded. After a long tirade at the engineer in charge he eventually shut up with "Please explain at once". The engineer tried very hard to convince him what was wrong but the chief would have none of it and demanded we set the crane back to the second beam in place, and lift it back up and 'he' would show them how to set it in place correctly. Not being involved, we just did as we were told and set the crane back, and after the beam was unbolted, lifted it up in the air; luckily, the glue was very slow setting. Then the chief started to line the beam up. After two hours he gave up and it ended up back down where it had been in the first place. He stomped off into the distance with a muttered command of "Get the rest down the best you can", which we did, just managing to get off site by the required 05.00hrs. So next time you travel along that stretch of line heading northwards from Darlington, keep an eye out of the window and watch the beams on top of the viaduct waver back and forth as you pass.

Tursdale (North of Ferryhill) 29th November, 6th & 13th December 1980

We came across the Chief Civil Engineer several times on various bridges and he always had the knack of appearing when something was amiss. A bridge at Tursdale, on the main line north of Ferryhill, was no exception. It was a small bridge over a farmer's road and it was immediately after, and joined to, a brick built bridge over a stream. Most of the short bridges over farmers' access to fields had been installed by the LNER and were simply made of old bullhead rails bolted together, put into place on the brick piers and then concrete poured over them. These bridges had been in place for a long time and doubt was now felt about their suitability for carrying today's modern high speed trains and heavy axle loads. Tursdale was to be renewed so that the internal condition could be assessed and therefore decide whether to renew all the others.

The site meeting had been a normal event with no problems envisaged. The crane was to stand on the brick bridge over the stream (with the civil engineer's permission), and once placed to their mark, the rails would be removed in front of the crane, the ballast removed, and after cutting the concrete into sections, half of the old bridge would be removed by the crane. The other mainline was left in place for the wagons containing equipment and the new bridge sections to stand on, the other half of the bridge being dealt with in the same manner the following weekend. I was told that the second weekend would have a female civil engineer trainee on site and would I ask my gang to be polite and very circumspect with their language, so as not to offend her.

Renewing the second half of the bridge at Tursdale. The crane is lifting the parapet section.

TAKING THE WEIGHT

On the following Saturday we arrived, after remarshalling at Ferryhill yard, at a cold and snowy site. After propelling with the crane leading, setting the crane to the engineer's mark, we lifted the relieving bogie down into the field below, then piled into the van for a cup of tea. An hour later a thump on the side of the van meant we were needed. Getting back to the crane we found the track had been cut and there was barely a foot between the burnt off end and the wheel of the crane, not exactly what I had expected. Once the rails and ballast had been removed we were required to lift a huge petrol driven diamond saw up from a lorry below and onto the uncovered bridge deck. This didn't take long and while the gang went back for another cup of tea, I sat on the crane and watched proceedings. It soon became apparent that the saw wasn't up to the task and it took longer than expected to cut the deck into two pieces for us to lift out. Again, there was a deadline of 05.00hrs on the Monday morning, which according to the plan, with an overrun allowance of 10 hours, was achievable, but this delay made it probable that the bridge wasn't going to be finished in time. Just as the final cut was finished their chief arrived on site and proceeded to chew everyone out over the lost time and then off he went again with "I'll be back". We lifted the first piece of decking up and loaded it into an adjacent wagon, and then tried to lift the other piece, but it didn't want to come up, so the engineers had to get in with pneumatic hammers and remove more concrete around the edges before it came free, so even more time was lost. This piece of decking needed a centre piece burning out so that it could be analysed as to whether any other bridges needed doing (after later renewing quite a few similar bridges, the answer was obviously yes). By now it was early morning and the sun was up and warming the air. We could now have our breakfast while the civil gang squared up the bridge footings and installed bearings for the new deck to sit on, so we were okay for a few hours to get some food and sleep.

At about lunch time they were ready, so the new deck was lifted out of its wagon and swung above its resting point. A few shovels of mortar were laid on the bearings, which is when I was introduced to a Thornaby tool van custom, as Dave Lindsay went down and tossed a penny onto the mortar, for good luck to all those who travelled over the bridge, he explained. As usual we spent ages getting the deck into the exact required position, and finally, after an hour it was down. After more preparation, the next task was to lift the parapet into place. This was glued and bolted onto the deck but the holes didn't line up enough for the long stainless steel studs to pass through. We found this out just as the chief appeared on the horizon, but at least this time he couldn't blame the people on site. Much head scratching later, they decided to carefully open the holes out, which took a long time, then when the studs were knocked through, one of the threads was damaged in the process. Much shouting then as the die, needed to repair the thread, had been left in the workshop at Newcastle, a fitter being dispatched post haste to get it. At long last the studs were in place and the nuts tightened to a specified torque, and we could release the parapet from the crane chains. It was then approaching 22.00 hrs and the chief decided to go as the difficult bit was over. But there was still a lot of work to do, as the deck and parapet had to be covered with fibre glass sheets and finally coated with a special compound to protect the concrete from the ballast and weather. This was a two pack compound, or should I say two barrel compound, which was mixed on site, but they ran out with only three quarters of the deck covered. Much more screaming ensued as a van raced off to another site to get more. Once fully coated, a few hours had to pass while it cured. It was, by then, breaking dawn again so everyone stopped for breakfast while the compound cured.

The race was then on as the new ballast was dropped from a wagon and a large vibrating roller used to tamp it down. But 05.00 passed and it still wasn't ready for the track. The Leamside branch could be seen across the fields and a steady stream of passenger trains started to pass along it in both directions, as the branch line was used as a diversion from the mainline. At last we lifted a new section of track back into place, which was temporarily fitted with fishplates. Before we could start putting the crane back together and the jib away, the plant the civils had been using had to be lifted and dropped down to waiting lorries on the farm track below, so it was 11.00 before we were ready to leave. For some reason we went back via Darlington and spent some hours in the up sidings waiting for a path, eventually arriving back at the shed some 36 hours after we had left.

The following weekend we were back at Tursdale on the opposite track, and this time things went a bit more smoothly. The female engineer had been put in charge and all the lads were very well behaved, and even when someone hit their hand with a hammer not a bad word passed his lips! A better saw was used this time, so the old deck was cut in two quickly and the two halves lifted out and into a wagon. We had a late dinner whilst the bridge supports were made ready, and a few hours later we got the call to lift the new deck into place. Again, a penny was thrown into the mortar and the deck lowered into place. It had to match the previously placed deck exactly, as holes had to line up for very long studs to pass through, so this took sometime, but eventually she was satisfied and we could let go of the deck. We all sat on the end of the crane as the civil engineering staff manoeuvred the long studs into position and pushed them through one by one. Well that was the plan. The first one went in, but the second would only go half way through before snagging, and after several tries the trainee engineer let fly with some very strong words. The whole job stopped, as everyone stared at her for several seconds, which caused more choice words designed to get people working again, which they certainly did. One could feel the stress lift after everyone being careful of their how they spoke, and all reverted to their normal language usage. As one of my lads said as we sat and watched "I didn't believe such a pretty girl could say such things". She quickly decided that the studs that jammed would be hammered through, and this time they had the die to run the threads down, so not much time was lost. The chief appeared just as the last nut was being tightened, and everyone breathed a sigh of relief that he hadn't appeared an hour earlier. He even complemented her on getting the job done on time. If only he knew what had gone on! This time the parapet lined up perfectly and there was enough compound, so by 02.00hrs the ballast was in place, the track dropped in and secured, and we were off site at 04.45, no doubt with a passenger train hard on our heels.

Bridlington Station Bridge 12th December 1982

The renewal of the road bridge over the west end of Bridlington Station was a case of treading on the toes of another Tool van area. Bridlington was actually in Doncaster's crane area, so when I got a call asking me to attend a site meeting at Bridlington I said straight away "But what about Doncaster?". Seemingly the civil engineers had looked at the crane diagrams and figured out that our 45 ton crane had a four foot longer reach with the jib than the 76 tonne crane of Doncaster and the 76T crane wouldn't do the job within the room available.

I thought there would be bother as this bridge would take four full weekends to renew. Sure enough, next day I had the Doncaster Supervisor on the phone complaining, but all I could say was take it up with the engineers and convince them your crane can do it. The next ploy was to try and get permission for them to use our crane, but our depot manager wouldn't have that as they weren't trained on our crane. Their final effort was to claim for loss of earnings ie the time they had lost, but their depot engineer knocked that on the head. As I've said, tool van men would try anything not to lose a job. I have lost some derailments to other tool vans, due to control calling the wrong vans, and claimed for my crew and usually won so we all got paid for not doing a job!!! Those were the days.

The actual job was interesting as the bridge had to be renewed in four segments, one each weekend. The tool vans left Thornaby at 5pm each Saturday via York and Selby so that we arrived at Bridlington as the last train left. Due to the site limitations our loco placed the crane roughly in position and then went back onto the vans, and the crew shut it down and left. Raising the jib we uncoupled the jib runner and relieving bogie, and pushed them well clear.

The old bridge was made of bow girders with a cross girder deck. The civils had already removed the deck so the two bow girders were sat in splendid isolation held down by a few ties. The civils had also burnt two holes in the top of the girder for us to put our chains through, but how to do that was the problem, no ladders long enough and I didn't fancy putting any side push on them anyway. One of the tool van lads, Dick Watson, answered that by climbing up the girder, then walking along the top web and looping each chain through the holes before calmly walking back down. It had been estimated that each girder weighed 35 tons so I made sure the crane was well packed. We were picking the girder up at a height of 16 feet so if anything went wrong the girder and crane had a long way to fall!! Of course the crane took the load as if there was nothing there. There wasn't much room to manoeuvre the girder, and there was only one civil engineer with us at that point to advise us as to what was wanted, so it was slowly spun round and lowered between the bridge supports onto the ground, then turned carefully onto its side and placed on a waiting wagon

TAKING THE WEIGHT

to be taken to a nearby yard for cutting up into manageable pieces. By then more civil engineering staff had turned up and they started getting the bridge piers ready for the new bridge sections, this was our cue to go and get a meal and some rest.

Several hours later a knock on the van side told me they were ready and out we trooped to continue. We had to pick up several concrete beams one at a time from rail wagons and place them carefully in position to within a millimetre on the new bed. Again, it took some juggling with the crane within the limited space, but these beams were light at 12 tons and we could move the crane whilst carrying them if needed. Once the beams were in place we manhandled the relieving bogies and jib wagon back onto the crane, put the crane away and returned to the riding van for a sleep. A few hours later I heard the class 40 start up and went out to tell the crew what was needed to re-marshall the train back into formation. Once back in the van all of us slept as we returned to Thornaby, again via Selby and York. We had to stand in York for a few hours to avoid the Monday morning rush hour which meant we got back to the shed around 10am. A 41 hour shift, not bad for the pay packet.

The other three weekends were virtual repeats of the first so we got into a routine, but there were times when the crane had to move into a different road for the lifts. This was accomplished by me driving the crane under its own power under the direction of the signalman, and using the fixed signals, but luckily I knew what the signals meant!

Derailments.

It would be boring to list all the derailments I have dealt with, so I will just mention those that were big or unusual or stick in my mind, along with the strange things that happened amongst what was a close knit group of men. No doubt there will be some I've missed!! There is no chronological order to these reminiscences.

Pull and be damned

Pulling back vehicles the way they had come was a method often used and allowed for in the little blue B.R. book, but the P'way department frowned on this method of re-railing, as they said it caused even more damage to the track, but sometimes there was no other way, and it could be quick. A case in point happened at Hartlepool in Newburn sidings, Cliff House. A class 37 had been going along the engine release line from the yard onto the slow line when the track gave way on a curve, so the loco ploughed down through the ballast and ended up off all wheels with the nearest good track about 20 feet directly behind it, and no tracks anywhere near it to the side.

What you could find awaiting you!   Dick Watson

A further explanation is needed when referring to most derailments in the Hartlepool area, in that the drivers stationed there were on a form of piece work, so that the quicker they got coal trains from place to place, the more they got paid, plus of course finishing early. (The Hartlepool area was known to the tool van men as the Gold Coast, due to the large number of derailments and therefore overtime payments to them).

As I stared at the mess, Dave Lindsay whispered, "Pull it back on" (he wanted to go out that night!) so after a think we set up to do just that. We took our class 37 off the tool vans and positioned it on the end of the good bit of track the derailed loco had just left. It took two of our long wire ropes shackled together to reach the drawbar of the derailed loco. Instructing our driver to drive from the rear cab, we gave it a tug, nothing happened, not even a twitch, it was up to its axles in mud. "Well, we will have to jack it" I said, but fate intervened, as another class 37 arrived in the yard and Dave soon had it hung on to our loco as well. Another tug with 3,500hp, and nothing, just wheelslip, so we uncoupled the pair of 37s, took them out and

TAKING THE WEIGHT

came back in with all the sanders working, so the rail top was awash with sand, coupled the cable back on and gave another tug, at which the 37 in the mud moved slightly then settled back. We'll put a bit of slack into the cable and give a running tug at it, was the next idea, so the loco's moved away at full throttle and snatched at the cable. The result was to prove to the driver that it had been a good idea to go to the opposite end cab, as the wire rope broke and neatly curved through the air, the end smashing through the centre cab window.

The fight was now on, there was no way that we would give in and use jacks!! Another wire rope was brought out and coupled up, and another snatch moved the loco a couple of feet through the mud. Just then the yard pilot a 350hp shunter (08) appeared, and was hung on to the 37s so we now had another extra 350hp, plus, by putting the traction motors into series the 08s would pull anything, (albeit slowly). So with the instruction to the three drivers to give it all they had, I waved them off. The derailed loco slowly started to move, and to my amazement accelerated. The plan had been to stop just as it got to the good track so we could check the alignment before proceeding further, though we had put some timber down ready to start guiding the wheels up and onto the track. The loco was now travelling at a good five miles an hour through the mud and ballast and before I could think, the wheels had reached and gone up the wood to the rail ends, and bounced up onto them. I had reacted by waving the loco's to stop pulling at that point, but Dave screaming "Keep it going as at least we will have it near some rails at last", made me wave the drivers on, the lads putting pieces of wood in place as each pair of wheels hit the rail ends and bounced onto the track. As the last pair came on I stopped the hauling loco's and the muddy 37 glided to a halt. We just stood and stared at this, as what had happened was just plain impossible. We had pulled loco's before and bogies just did their own thing, certainly never staying in line with the track when buried in mud or lifting up to rail height on just a few bits of timber. But we had re-railed a loco that was thirty feet away from the track end in just under two hours, there was no more damage to the loco or the track other than that which had been caused by the original derailment, and Dave got his night out. Though I'm not sure how we explained the broken window!!

In contrast, 60092 was driven back on when loco's were more sophisticated and computer controlled. This had split the points in the grid sidings at Lackenby (Steelworks) and ended up off all wheels. The ground conditions were very poor and jacking it up would have been difficult or even dangerous. I elected to drive it back on, much to the British Steel P'way Supervisor's dismay. He went away muttering we would have to pay for all damage done. We always had a large box of broken hard wood packing timbers in the packing van and lorry which were always full to the top, so this timber was used to pack between the rails as they came together at the point blades, and then lots of complete different thickness packing timbers were used, with the aim of lifting the wheels to rail height as they moved along. Having told everyone what to do (they knew anyway), as there were no drivers there (because we had come with the road rail vehicle and lorry), I got into the cab. Putting the loco into slow speed at 0.5mph we slowly moved along, and using the packing correctly, the wheels slowly came up to height just as the rails came together at the points and dropped onto the rails. Again, what would have taken hours using jacks was accomplished in 45 minutes with no damage to the track or loco, the only casualties being to some of the wood packing.

Hearing that the loco had been re-railed quickly the P'way Supervisor came rushing back to look for damage to his track, but of course he didn't find any, much to his chagrin. The beauty of the class 60 was that the computer controlled slow speed system kept the loco at a steady 0.5mph and if any wheel wasn't in contact with the packing or the ground then power was removed from that motor until it did grip. Some of the old hands complained it was moving too slowly, as they were waiting for a particular wheel to get to a point where it needed a bit more wood, but older designs of loco's if driven could be a problem, as they would be moving too fast with no control over spinning wheels.

Coal for the people

Just as Hartlepool was the Gold Coast to us, the line to East Hetton Colliery was a place we regularly visited, but for some strange reason, for some months in 1977 we virtually went every Friday afternoon. The colliery sidings were at the top of the single line branch up from Ferryhill and about a half mile from the top was a catch point. The usual call was to re-rail a dozen or so 21 ton loaded hopper wagons which had run away from the sidings and down to the catch point. The cause always given to us for our records was colliery shunters error!! Without fail during this period one could expect the phone to ring at about 15.00hrs and off we would go, re-marshal the train at Ferryhill yard to have the crane leading, and propel up to the derailment, a distance of about five miles. Once there the jib runner and relieving bogie would be lifted out of the way onto the lineside, and the crane moved right up to the wagons where we would pick them up and put them on a long siding, which luckily came down from the colliery so that their loco could pick them up. As we got used to the regular calls, someone suggested that we leave the packing for the beams in place, which we did, and when we went back the next time, sure enough, it was possible to set the crane straight back onto the packing. This saved much carrying back and forth, but eventually we stopped going as much so I had to send a road van to recover the packing. There were rumours at the depot that one of the tool van men paid the colliery shunters to let the wagons go down the bank so we got guaranteed overtime, but I think the truth was more likely to be kids letting the wagon brakes off, and when the wagons derailed the local population would have free coal from all the spillage.

Never a scout around when you need one...

As part of trials to modernise (sic) the way derailments were handled, in late February 1977 I was asked to go up to Newcastle to meet up with several bigwigs (sorry, senior officers) at the North Eastern Region Headquarters based in Irving House. I cannot remember everyone who was there, but Reeves, Bellwood, Bird and Crosby spring to mind. It was cold and pouring down as we all piled into two huge saloon cars and headed up the Tyne valley to a small station called Riding Mill. Arriving in the very large station car park we were met by a technical assistant, who had driven up earlier with a large trailer tent and some boxes. The object of the exercise was to see if the tent, along with a portable cooker, walkie-talkies and other items long forgotten, would be of use as an incident centre.

So an interesting few hours were spent trying to get the tent up in the pouring rain and then making tea with the small gas range. Being the youngest (and it was raining) I was sent out to walk away from the tent with one of the walkie-talkies to see what its range was. According to the box it should have been half a mile, but we found out that I had only gone a hundred yards or so when it petered out. Getting back to the tent, the kettle was barely warm and one of the officers had the brainwave of "Let's stop this stupidity and go to the pub" which was just outside the gate. So the next couple of hours were spent with a pie and a pint listening to the officers of the railway talking about things that (a) I didn't understand and (b) I shouldn't have been party to. The next good idea was to get back to Newcastle, which we did, leaving the poor technical assistant to pack the tent up and get everything back to headquarters. The post script to this was that a few months later a van arrived at Thornaby towing the trailer tent complete with cooker etc. A later phone call explained that as I had seen it all in use it had been decided to base it at Thornaby for my use!! The tent, as far as I am aware, was only ever raised once more, when we had a naming ceremony at Thornaby for a loco, and it was used as a hospitality area. It then hung around for a few more years before being bought for a pittance by a member of staff who certainly got more use from it than the railway ever did.

Assisting Gateshead at Consett   8th February 1979

We had a booked call to go to Consett to assist Gateshead to re-rail 37037 which had derailed at a head shunt buffer stop. It took a few hours to get up to Consett and there was a blizzard raging as we pulled into the yard. Frank Beattie, the Gateshead Supervisor, met us and explained that we needed to marshal the crane to be the trailing vehicle. This done, we set off out of the yard and onto the remains of the Blackhill Branch. This part of the line was on a steep gradient as soon as it left Consett yard, and as we went down we could see the head shunt line falling at a lesser gradient so that it was getting higher in relation to us the further we went. After travelling a half of a mile we came to the loco. The driver had thought he was on the branch line when really he was on the head shunt line and by the time he realised his mistake, it was too late and the loco smashed through the buffers and down the drop after the track end. Frank had arranged that we would be downhill of the loco, with the Gateshead crane uphill of it. Firstly, we had to lift the remains of the buffer stop out of the way, while Gateshead made the best of putting their slides out, as the headshunt embankment wall stopped them getting them out fully.

37037 looking sorry at Consett   Bill Flower

Due to the nature of the site, Frank couldn't control both cranes, so we both discussed the plan of action and looked after our own lift. The first part was very difficult as we were lifting the lowest part of the loco, and initially the heaviest part of the lift, but our 45 ton crane didn't budge an inch as it lifted the loco. Once we had floated the loco at our end, Gateshead could lift their end until clear. Then both cranes slewed around so that the loco, still at an angle between the cranes was clear of the headshunt, then Gateshead could lower their end and take the strain off both cranes before again slewing round so that the loco was above the track between the cranes and finally placed on the track. Some fine measurement had taken place as the loco fitted between the cranes with a couple of inches to spare! A very difficult job that took about four hours from start to finish, but luckily the snow had stopped and a bright winter sun shone down on us. All the time we had the loco lifted, I was trying to figure out what the load was on each crane hook, but with the cranes sat on a steep gradient to start with, I gave up and thanked Cowan & Sheldon for building two tough resilient cranes.

Going Fishing

A call to Hall Dene level crossing on the morning of 10th September 1979 meant me learning a new trick. The derailment was actually in Gateshead's area but their crane was on repairs and they only had their MFD jacks. A loaded coal train composed of 21 ton hopper wagons travelling south, had come off just before the level crossing and then proceeded to scatter itself around the railway when it came to the point work that led to Vane Tempest Colliery sidings. Gateshead had already arrived at the north end and was busy re-railing a couple of wagons with MFD jacks on their side of the level crossing, where the track wasn't too badly damaged. Our side of the level crossing was a different picture as there was a heap of wagons where the points had been, and coal everywhere. Luckily the sidings for the transfer point to the colliery were just there by the side of us.

Propelling the crane up to the heap, we lifted the jib runner and then the relieving bogie out of the way and moved the crane in as near as we could. Putting the crane in close meant that several wagons could be lifted without having to reset the crane, another point that one soon learnt. The crane made short work of dealing with the closest wagons even though they were tangled up together. Either a little pull and jiggle left or right, or a straight forward pull to tear them out, soon had a wagon in the air. They could then be put on a track close by, until we could reach no more. After checking the track in front was still good enough to go over, the crane once more moved into the remains of the heap. Within a few hours all the wagons had been re-railed except one, which was just by the level crossing, stood upright on its own, but no track for about 100ft between it and the crane. Mr Crosby, the On Call Engineer had been on site most of the time but had not interfered with our plans or method of work until now. As we looked at the wagon, the distance, and the possibilities of getting the track put right to get the crane near, he came up to me and said, " Don't try getting that wagon until the track is fixed. I'll go and get the P'way to come and get started", and off he went (no mobile phones in those days!!).

So we went to the riding van and had a rest and a bite to eat. An hour later there was no sign of anyone so we had another look at the wagon and the distance. I was looking for some means of pulling the wagon nearer (as unlike modern cranes we didn't have a winch), when Dave suggested that if we dropped the jib down low and manually pulled the block as far as we could, and then use some loose wire ropes, we might just reach the draw hook of the wagon. We set to, and after a lot of hard work had the jib down and the main hook on the floor pulled towards the wagon. Shackling several wire ropes together we managed to get the end rope onto the drawbar. Dave then climbed into the cab of the crane shouting "I'm going fishing". First the jib was lifted, which took all the slack up in the ropes, and whilst pulling at the wagon, provided a small amount of lift at the same time, so the wagon started to move towards us when enough pull was there. I should mention that the jib gearing is much more powerful than the main hook gearing, so if you couldn't lift using the main hook, then lifting with the jib would pick anything up. Also, the crane was end on to the wagon, therefore at its most stable, the loco and several coaches with the brakes hard on behind the crane stopped it moving to the wagon. Once the jib was right up so that the wagon was starting to be lifted high at one end, the jib was lowered, some wire ropes removed and the process repeated. In a way it was as Dave had said, just like pulling a fish in with a rod and line. After four pulls like this the wagon could be lifted within a few minutes, and the wagon was pushed into the sidings with the rest of them. We set back and lifted the relieving bogie and jib runner back onto the track, coupled them up, put the crane away, and were just tidying up the packing etc. when Mr Crosby hove into view. He had a few choice words with me about getting the wagon close to the crane and re-railed when he had said not to, but he never asked how we had done it! He hadn't been able to get the P'way interested in sorting the track just for the crane as they were aiming to come during the night and sort the whole junction out in one go. So I think he was secretly relieved that we had got the job done and the tool vans were nearly ready to go back to the shed.

Class 37s in a muddy hole 24th September 1979

Most big derailments seem to happen when weather conditions are far from ideal. On 24th September 1979 two class 37s, 37098 & 37053 came to grief at South Pelaw, at the bottom of the steep gradient from Consett, as there was heavy rain. The train had been returning with empty 100 ton iron ore wagons, and just as it approached South Pelaw junction, one of the tyres on the first pair of wheels on the leading loco 37098 came off its wheel. This resulted in both loco's and the first couple of wagons derailing at speed, the end result being that the leading loco actually spun around 180 degrees losing its bogies, in the process demolishing the junction track work and digging a large muddy hole for itself, and the following loco ended up more or less alongside it.

We got the call to go in the afternoon and travelled to Ferryhill, and then onto the now defunct 'Leamside branch' up to Washington. There we re-marshalled the train so that the crane was leading back up to South Pelaw, and propelled the train up to the site of the derailment. Mr Reeves, the Newcastle Divisional Maintenance Engineer, had gone straight there to assess the job, he had also sent for Doncaster's 76 tonne crane (as Gateshead's was on repairs) which had arrived a short time before us. Gateshead was also there with their rail vans dealing with the derailed wagons, using their MFD jacking gear. So the two cranes were stood facing each other, more or less alongside the leading loco sat in its muddy hole, with the bogies still more or less underneath but displaced. Mr Reeves explained that we would have to lift that loco up first and put it on the track between the cranes, and then Doncaster crane would have to move back with the loco, put it in a nearby siding, and then come down the remaining bit of track so their crane was end on to the other loco. Meanwhile, we would go back to Washington, re-marshal the train and go to Tyne Yard via Washington, North Pelaw and Gateshead, re-marshal the train to have the crane at the front again and propel up from Tyne Yard to South Pelaw on the remaining main line so we were at the other end of the loco. After explaining the plan to me and the Doncaster Supervisor, Mr Reeves said he had a meeting to go to but he would be back at eight in the morning and he expected the first loco to be on, and off he went!!

As we looked at the locos spread in disarray before us, I said to the Doncaster Supervisor, "Well according to the 'Crane Manual', on dual lifts with two cranes the Supervisor of the largest capacity crane is in charge of the operations". "Hmm" he said "but I have never done a crane job on my own as I've just passed out and got my certificate"!!! So the onus was on me, again. The first lift was way out of range of our 20' radius and 45 ton lift capacity, and was nearer 30 foot radius with 35 tons capacity, plus the weight on our hook was going to be in the region of 55 tons, though the bogie wouldn't be lifted straight away, giving us approximately 40 tons to start with. So I instructed both cranes to lift their runners and relieving bogies out of the way, and then I would set the 45 ton crane first and the 76 tonne could be set a loco length away. The rain was still pouring down and it was pitch black by then. We had as many floodlights out as we could muster and thankfully the 76 tonne crane lights were working, which was a big help.

Once the cranes were set, they were slewed round and the wire ropes attached to the lifting brackets. Being over our limit of lift we took the weight a few times to settle the packing and repack the slides. I then took control of both cranes and they slowly lifted the loco, which came up straight away. Both cranes stood firm with no sign of movement at all, but once up in the air the problems of the bogies had to be solved. This is where the Doncaster Supervisor came into his own as he had seen something similar a few months previous. He suggested that a large four leg chain be placed with the centre ring in the middle of the cab floor and two legs out of each cab door then hooked onto the bogie. Having lowered the loco down as close to the bogies as possible, we put the long chains on to shortening clutches then they would lift the bogies straight away. Again the cranes lifted without any problems, and the loco now with its bogies hanging from the chains, slowly came around towards the rails and was very quickly in line between the cranes. One bogie at a time was lowered onto the track and the body left in the air, whilst the bogies were made fit for the body to be reunited, then the body was lowered onto them. We must have measured the distance between the cranes properly as we had 6 inches to spare once the loco was on the track between them. When the bogies were in place and once more fastened to the body, we lifted the loco with its bogies and fitted a wheelskate under the wheelset with the loose tyre, so that it could be safely moved once more on the rails. Once that was achieved we soon had the crane put away for travelling. As we were coming back we left all our packing and lights etc. on site and then headed to Washington, then to Tyne Yard via the bridges over the Tyne so that the crane would be jib first up to South Pelaw and onto the opposite line to where we had been. This gave us plenty of chance to get some hot food and a sleep before starting all over again.

Several hours later, a bang on the side of the coach to say we had arrived woke me up from my slumbers (being on the tool vans gave one the ability to sleep anywhere at any time and to eat at irregular intervals). The Doncaster crane was already set up and the wire ropes attached to the lifting brackets of the remaining loco and the gang was fast asleep in their van. So we soon had our crane in place and ready to lift as well, and before waking the Doncaster lads up we decided, as it was eight-o-clock, to have a tea break. Just as we were climbing into the van Mr Reeves appeared, he was pleased with our progress and had a cup and a chat as well. Lifting this loco was a bit more difficult as we had to reach a bit further to get the first lift (in the region of 60 tons on the hook of our 45 ton crane at radius that only allowed about 30 tons) and it took a while to get the packing to settle so the crane was stable. Once we had it floating in the air we could bring the jib up, whilst Doncaster came out on their jib, and the loco was soon slewed around and onto the track in front of us. All that remained then was to put everything away, which on such a big job took some time, say goodbye to our Doncaster mates (for now... see the Bridlington bridge episode!) and set off for Tyne Yard with the loco, re-marshal and head for Thornaby and home for tea.

Supervising Gateshead Tool vans

In the late 70s I had been given some training and passed out on the 76 tonne diesel converted steam crane based at Gateshead depot, so that I could cover for the Supervisor there. Frankie Beattie was on holiday and for some reason there was no longer a relief for Frank. I was only ever called once, and this was, to my disbelief, for a bridging job at Alnmouth on the 10th March 1979. Getting to Gateshead for 21.00 on the Saturday night I found the vans all ready to go. In contrast to Thornaby's vans, these had all mod cons and were up to date conversions of MK1 coaches. Climbing into the riding van it was obvious that I wasn't going to be greeted with open arms as I went through to the Supervisor's compartment watched by sullen silent faces. I was no substitute for Frank, and of course there was the language barrier. The Geordie accent was difficult to understand, especially at a working man's level when you had to get technical things across. After all, I was a southerner from only 36 miles away with a totally different accent. The cook was okay, he spoke when he brought a cup of hot tea and a large plateful of Sunday lunch through for me. Obviously no expense spared in the food department at Gateshead, they certainly took the tool van maxim to heart 'Eat and sleep when you can because you don't know when you may next get the chance'.

A couple of hours later we had arrived. It was a small over bridge for a farmer to use. I hadn't been to the site meeting but the engineer on site there explained it was a simple case of lifting the old bridge off in one lump and dropping a new one into place and everything was ready. Because of the nature of the job there was no need to split the train, just drop the relieving bogies down and two front slides out and packed. The first problem was getting the gang to do something, but that was eased by the fact that Gateshead vans had a charge fitter (Alec Taylor). I took him aside and said "I know you don't want me here but here I am, so you get the crane all set up and ready to lift, and I'll only interfere if I don't like what I see". At that, he went off, and the gang burst into life, and before I knew it flood lights were out, the slides packed and the jib up in the air ready for action. A rail wagon was alongside and all we had to do was sling the old bridge and lift it into the wagon, then when the civils had made the bridge pillars ready for the replacement, we then lifted the new bridge section out of another wagon and dropped it into place. Alec came up with a two way radio and said "Here you'll need this, you're the boss, and you're in charge of the crane". So I took charge of the crane telling the driver what I wanted, no whistles and hand signals here. Being a simple bridge, the job was completed relatively quickly and by 10.00 hours the bridge was finished ready for the farmer and his cows. I was just about to get Alec to put the crane away, (not an easy thing if you didn't know what you were doing), when an operating Supervisor appeared and said, "Good, you're on time, if you're ready we'll set back and fill these wagons with scrap". Sure enough some wagons had appeared further back in a siding off the loop. Frank had omitted to tell me, that while we were at Alnmouth there were some old wagons in a siding to finish cutting up and lift into some 16 ton mineral wagons. So we went back into the loop and spent some hours loading lumps of dismantled wagon into the waiting wagons. Good practice for the two Gateshead lads who did the burning; at least it was a beautiful warm sunny day.

At long last, late on the Sunday afternoon, I asked Alec to put the crane away as I did the paperwork, and lo and behold the operating Supervisor appeared again, this time with a message that we had to go to Newcastle Central station where a parcels van was derailed both bogies in the centre roads. Once the vans were ready to move we shot off south, the train crew obviously wanted to get back home. The Gateshead tool vans and crane had a maximum speed of 60 mph and we certainly achieved that on the way back to Newcastle. Arriving alongside the derailed van the Gateshead lads stood waiting to see what I would make of this, as we couldn't use the crane under the station roof. I was on territory I knew now and said "Right, two short beams, trolleys and 120 ton jacks" which duly appeared. Once I explained what I wanted they got down to the job, I think they had finally accepted I knew what I was doing as it didn't take long to lift one end, which was when the fun started. "Right, lets push this end over then" I said, and out of the jacking van appeared a 4 ton Pul-lift (a type of chain hoist operated by a hand lever), a few chains and a homemade attachment, which dropped into the socket of the trolley to be pulled across. They were just going to start setting the Pul-lift up when I said "Whoa, what on earth are you doing?" "Pulling the trolley across as you asked" came the reply. "Not with that" I said "Where's your Push Pull jack?" "Oh we never use that" they said, "Frank doesn't like them". "I am tired and want to get home soon, it will take ages with that thing you have" I replied. "Now get the Push Pull!!" Sheepishly one of them went and got the jack, still in its protective coating, brand new, never used, "We don't know how to use it" was the next retort, so I grabbed the jack and dropped it into place and told the jack operator to lift slowly. As the trolley glided along the beam they just looked, and after I had reset it a few times they were converted and fell over themselves to do the other end. There was no way they were going to use the Pul-lift method again. The van was re-railed quickly and when we parted company back at the depot we were all old pals and I looked forward to working with them again, but unfortunately it never happened.

Damage York Station?? Not Me Sir! 18th January 1983

Doncaster crane was out on another job, so early one evening we got a call to York Station where some over enthusiastic shunting had propelled E86342, a 57' parcels van, over a buffer stop in the East Bay, platform 1. Arriving at about 21.00 in platform 8 we walked over and weighed the job up. The van had leapt up into the air leaving its bogies on the rails and the body was sat halfway over the buffer stop and onto the platform. After a discussion with the night Station Supervisor we left the tool vans in platform 2 opposite the derailed van and propelled the crane into the bay, up to the van. We were just inside the limit for reaching out and picking the body up in one lift, but that's when the problems started. The bay was on a curve, which meant slewing the crane to the left. This meant that the backend of the crane would have to go past the boundary fence. It was a wire fence which separated the line from the car park and there were only a few cars parked there. Exactly where the backend of the crane would go, was parked a Rolls Royce!

Parcel van at, oops sorry, on York Station   Dick Watson

The Station Supervisor was happy for us to cut the fence as he wanted the van removed before the public arrived for the morning rush hour, but the Rolls Royce was another thing all together. Having the backend of the crane sat dropping hot ash and dribbling hot water and oil all over it didn't bear thinking about, so the British Transport Police were called. Two officers arrived, scratched their heads and pondered, and soon had the owner's phone number. On ringing him they found that he was in a hotel in Scarborough and there was no way he was going to help move his Rolls out of the way. After more head scratching, the next thing I know is the Station Supervisor and the policemen arrive with a wagon sheet, which was carefully draped over the Rolls, and we had the nod to get started. Within a few hours we had lifted the van and moved back with it hanging from the lifting beam so that we could position it and set the bogies back to their rightful positions before lowering the body down onto them, which is where the problems continued. The previously nice Station Supervisor was soon to become my enemy. As we slewed right to get the van positioned correctly, the back of the crane roof just came into contact with the fancy cast iron valance of the platform awning and brought a section crashing to the ground. I think I learnt a few new words from the Supervisor, as he went berserk and accused me of wilful damage to his beloved station, and I was threatened with having to pay to get it replaced and other such things. He said he would write to my Depot Manager and get me sacked.

Another view showing the awning valance   Dick Watson

Of course, I never heard another thing about it, and since that day, every time I passed through York station I always smiled at the missing valance which looked like a few teeth missing! But when I went through in late 2006, I noticed that it had been replaced, with probably a resin copy. Once the van was back on its bogies we helped the policemen to carefully remove the sheet from the Rolls and we even repaired the fence so that as far as anyone was concerned nothing had ever been disturbed, let alone the tail end of a steam crane hanging over a Rolls dropping hot ash and oil on it!

To show how time passed in those days, the accident happened at 23.20, we were ordered at 00.50, left the depot at 01.50 and arrived York station at 05.00. Despite the Rolls Royce and not being an easy job, the parcels van was re-railed by 08.15, but we didn't leave York until 10.40 as we had to wait a path through the morning passenger trains, arriving back at the shed at 13.15hrs.

Scared of heights

Dave Crossley was a fitter's assistant who had been on the tool vans for some years, and one thing we found out was that he was scared of heights. We had been up to a derailment at South Pelaw and had gone via the Leamside branch and returned the same way. South of Washington there is a long viaduct (Victoria Viaduct) and we had at the time the combined jacking riding van. One of the lads had an idea about Dave and his phobia, so a plan was hatched that involved us all. As we approached the viaduct, which had a 20mph speed restriction on it, I said to Dave "Give me a hand to secure a jack that's come loose". As he came into the jacking area I had opened the sliding outer door where jacks were lifted in and out, and was looking over the viaduct edge at the valley below, the rest of the staff had crept in behind Dave, grabbed him, hustled him to the door and physically held him right out over the viaduct edge as we travelled along. Of course Dave screamed blue murder but he was held hanging over the edge until we reached the end of the viaduct, and then brought inside where he calmed down and eventually joined in the laughter. Strangely, the experience didn't cure his fear of heights, I don't know why.

The sliding door Dave was held out from L-R M Bielby, Jack Wickham, Jim Davison, George Singh and Ken Barwick (crouching)

I won't eat that

Another fitter's assistant was Jack Baldwin. Jack was a good worker, game for anything, and in the riding van would have strong views on all sorts of subjects, one of which was Indian food... Having George Singh and Mohammed Anwar on the crew, curry was a frequent request for a meal, but Jack would have none of this and said no way would he eat curry. On the way to a derailment we were held in every loop on the way, and the same coming back, so we were out for a long time. On the way there Bill Flower, the then cook, started to make what was commonly called 'Yuk Soup'. This consisted of tins of corned beef, potatoes, carrots, peas, 'Oxo' cubes and anything else that came to hand and thrown into a large pan!! Left cooking for a while, it was actually quite nourishing and filling, and no one ever complained about having it. The kitchen was next door to my compartment and suddenly the door opened and an arm appeared, waving a carton of curry powder, and then disappeared. On the way back, more 'Yuk soup' was made, and again this carton was waved in front of my eyes and disappeared again. Later in the week 'Yuk Soup' was again on the menu and, as before, the carton appeared through the door. After a few

TAKING THE WEIGHT

minutes I went into the kitchen and asked Bill what on earth was going on, "Follow me" he said, and went into the staff compartment and slammed the empty curry carton down on the table in front of Jack, who stared at it and quietly said "I've been eating curry haven't I?" "Of course" said Bill, "for the last week, and getting stronger each time, and you never said a word!" We had curry more often after that.

Getting our own back 20th March 1981

One morning we got a call that the Down line on the Ferryhill Branch at Stillington was obstructed and the crane was required. We were off the shed quickly and soon arrived to find a road crane on the point of sliding down the embankment edge. The embankment was wide at this location as it originally carried four tracks for all the coal traffic the line once carried. The road crane had been stolen by vandals during the night and driven along the embankment all the way from Simpasture until the embankment had started to narrow and the crane began to slip down the edge, so it had been abandoned there. The first train of the day had come along and found the crane in its precarious position, there being just enough room for the train to get by, and they had continued, reporting it to the signalman at Ferryhill. The owners, when notified, had tried to drive the crane backwards but it just kept slipping further off the edge of the embankment, thus we were called to see what we could do with it.

Old lifts the new

When we arrived we found the owner scratching his head as to how to get his crane back home. After a walk around, I thought the best way would be to grab hold of it around the four outriggers which would give us a square lift, then the crane should balance in the slings as well. Explaining to the owner what I intended to do, after another head scratch he said "That's fine". The crane weighed 12 tons so I had all the slides put out on our crane with single packing (which can be seen in the photo). Using the spreader beam with its four wire ropes we attached these to the road crane with nylon straps around its outriggers. Just as I was about to start lifting, the owner came rushing up and asked "Is your crane capable of lifting my crane?!" I just pointed at the 45 ton on the jib side and said nothing. "Oh" he said, and walked away.

I carefully lifted the road crane up to make sure it sat squarely and level in the slings, which it did, then took it high enough and jibbed out so we could spin it around to face the other way, then lowered it down as close to the railway as I could. Taking our slings off, the owner came up muttering about the welds on one of the outriggers being fractured, but when I mentioned he had agreed with the method of lifting he again shut up and went and started the crane up. We quickly put the crane away, and as we climbed into the riding van the road crane slowly drove away with a P'way ganger escorting him. The operating manager with us said we would have to stay there an hour as he needed to make sure the road crane had left the railway safely first, "Come in for a cuppa and a bacon bun then" I said.

L-R John Young (big John), Joe Glass, Yours truly, Owen Batey, George Singh

TAKING THE WEIGHT

Beef anyone? 5th April 1981

A call to a DMU derailed all wheels at Greatham was disturbing, as it was reported as having struck a cow. On arrival we found that it had hit several cows. Vandals had broken a fence down, the cows had wandered onto the line, and being dark the driver hadn't seen them until too late. The few passengers on board weren't hurt and had been walked back along the track to a safe point then put on a bus to carry on with their journey. A vet had been summoned and he had put down any cattle that were still alive. We used the crane to lift the unit one bogie at a time, and then cleared the carcasses from underneath; this wasn't easy as the cows were entangled with the bogies and undergear. This was a horrendous task, as the stench was terrible and where carcasses were entangled we had to resort to using a large saw to cut them up, with lots of tugging and heaving to get the bits out - cows aren't light. Later some 'Knackers Yard' men arrived and they made the job a little easier for us, though we had to get the bits out to start with. Even so, it took all night to clear the line in time for the first train of the day. After putting the crane away we climbed back onto the riding van to be met by Bill the cook saying "Fresh beef stew for you tonight lads", but before he could be lynched he produced fresh fish and chips which were soon devoured - tough breed tool van men.

Bang, and there it was, gone 4th July 1983

An unusual derailment was the day we went to South Stockton Goods Yard; all the sidings leading down to the goods yard were on a fairly steep incline from Bowesfield junction. To the right of the sidings, leading into the goods shed and loading area, was a single line coal staithes, with room for four coal wagons at a time. This particular day the shunter had drawn some two axle continental ferry wagons out of the goods shed and put them onto the top end of the line leading to the staithes. Unbeknown to him, the handbrakes he had applied on these wagons were virtually useless. When he came back with more wagons to couple to them, as soon as the buffers touched the ferry wagons they ran away towards the staithes where there were two 21 ton coal hopper wagons being unloaded by the coalman.

A balancing act at Stockton South Coal Staithes.   Dick Watson

TAKING THE WEIGHT

As the coalman later said to me, "I didn't hear a thing, one minute I was stood by the side of the coal wagon opening the doors and next there was a bang and it had gone, and I was left staring at a blue ferry van!!!!" The ferry vans had pushed the coal wagons through the buffer stop at the end of the staithes and left the first one upside down on the cobbled road, then the next one perfectly balanced on top of the first, with a ferry van hanging over the end of the rails against it. There was no access for any rail crane, so 'Whites' a local road crane firm just down the road was contacted. Their rep came to assess what size crane would be required, and after a quick measure said an 80 ton crane would be needed, which made me think, 80 tons?? Luckily, they had one spare in their yard, and a driver, so an hour later we had a nearly brand new crane at our disposal. A talk through with the crane driver as to what we would do, and he set about setting the crane up, which was a pleasure to watch, as one man, with the aid of hydraulics, easily set the beams out and packed the crane.

Road crane with no bells ringing!!   Dick Watson

Firstly we fastened the chains to the wagon balanced on top of the other and I signalled the crane driver to lift. As the crane began to lift and take the full weight, a bell began to ring and the lift stopped. "Can't lift that" he said "too heavy for the crane". "Err excuse me" I replied, "this is an 80 ton capacity crane and you're only lifting about 15 tons and it's too heavy?" "Well yes, it's an 80 ton crane but that's only with the jib straight up in the air, at this radius it can only pick up 10 ton". I was learning fast about road cranes. The radius of the road crane jib for picking the wagon up was about 35 feet. I pointed up the track to our crane stood in the siding, "That" I said "was built in 1940, 45 ton capacity, driven by steam, no mod cons, and it will pick up 30 tons at the radius this crane of yours is at". "Oh" he said "I'll see what I can do". He did something in the cab and started to lift again, no bell this time, and the wagon lifted clear with no obvious distress to the crane. The wagon was placed out of the way on the hard standing.

Next, the ferry van was picked up at one end and moved back so it was back on the track of the coal staithes. The wagon that was upside down was lifted as it was and placed in front of the crane. I told the driver that we would put the chains from the drawhook under a buffer and the corner of the body, and when we lifted it, would turn the wagon onto its side and then reset the chains and do the same again, and it would end up on its wheels. "Oh you can't do that" he said "it might shock load the crane". Again I pointed to our crane, "that old thing tears wagons out of heaps of wreckage ". "Well I'll see what happens" he said. So he did as I had asked, the crane didn't even give a shudder as the wagon turned over, the load on the chains slowly released each time. All that was to be done then was to pick up each wagon in turn and lift them back up onto the coal staithes track, where a loco was waiting to take them away. Half an hour later the crane had been put away and was gone, it was very neat and easy to use, but woefully lacking in capacity and stamina for something that was labelled 80 tons! As we walked back to the tool vans we passed the coalman who was shovelling away and cursing that the different types of coal had been mixed up in the staithes coal cells.

HST derailed Tyne Yard 1st August 1984

The scene that greeted us at Tyne Yard. That's me, arms folded looking down.
Dick Watson

We had heard a rumour that a High Speed train (HST) had derailed at Tyne Yard, but being in Gateshead's area, I didn't think too much of it until ten minutes later, when my phone rang with control saying Thornaby was required at Tyne Yard to a derailed HST. Gateshead couldn't go as their crane was off call for repairs. So we left the shed in record time, details were only sketchy but we were told to get there as soon as possible.

Arriving at the south end of Tyne Yard we ground to a halt on the Down goods, and after a few minutes the secondman was banging on the side of the van to tell me they couldn't get any further as the track was damaged, so off I set on foot, no HST in sight. After a few minutes' walk I could see the rear car of the HST in front of me, and after another five minutes' walk I'd reached it. I'd passed a set of points before I reached the power car and up to them the track looked perfect, but after them the track and sleepers were all chewed up and progressively getting worse. The derailment must have started at those points so the cause wouldn't be hard to find when the Railway Inspectorate arrived. (The cause was found to be loose bolts in the point stretcher bars which allowed the blades to move under the wheels). Getting to the rear power car, this was derailed all wheels, as were the next two coaches. The fourth coach had veered to the left and partially gone down an embankment, the fifth was on its side at the bottom of the embankment, the sixth was partially up the embankment, the seventh derailed one bogie and the eighth coach and leading power car were still on the rails.

Of course, by this time all the passengers had left the scene, there had been no serious injuries even in the coach on its side, a tribute to the modern design of coaches. There was hardly anyone about apart from a couple of P'way men, but then along strode Mr Reeves with Doug Moffat, Thornaby's Depot Engineer, and Phil Crosby the Maintenance Engineer at Thornaby. They had been on the train and had taken charge immediately. Realising that rail cranes couldn't get anywhere near, they had ordered two road cranes to the site. Within two hours we had received a 100 ton crane with a 160 ton crane following later, as that had burst a steering hose whilst fighting its way over Tyne Yard's rough ground to get to us. A gang from Gateshead's tool vans had already arrived by road and Frankie Beattie their Supervisor had them get to work using chain warricks to hold the track together under the coaches still on the track so they could be dragged away, meanwhile my gang had gone to fetch burning gear and packing etc. ready to start using the cranes.

The first road crane was set in position, my crew helping the driver to set up, which he appreciated, as normally he would do this on his own. The other crane still wasn't available so the 100T crane was used to lift all the visible loose coach bogies up and place them behind us for later. By that time the other crane (160T) had arrived, and this was set up ready with the 100T crane to lift the coach that was on its side at the bottom of the embankment. We had managed to get a nylon sling under the coach at a bogie centre line, and using the 160T crane the coach was turned upright and ended up nearer the cranes in the process. Meanwhile the Gateshead crew had come back, so there were two gangs of nine men, supervised by myself and Frankie Beattie. The crane held the coach in place while we

Lifting the coach up to the embankment.   Dick Watson

fitted the lifting brackets into their pockets at the bogie centre lines. We didn't need any packing as all the under gear had been torn off during the plunge down the bank. I should point out that the Senior Managers had left earlier, once they knew that things were in place to deal with the situation, with the promise they would be back to see how we were doing!

Once the two cranes had the lifting slings attached it was time to lift the coach up, which was when the road crane bug hit us. I stood between the cranes so that each driver could see me and controlled them using a hand for each (bit like playing a piano!). As soon as the 100T crane took the load the alarm bell started to ring, so the lift stopped!! Each crane was being asked to lift approximately 15T. Getting both crane drivers together, Frank and I asked "Where do we go from here??" "Need at least two 200T cranes mate" was the reply. Frank pointed down the track to my crane (which was now closer thank goodness) and said " That old steam crane of Bob's would pick the whole coach up without a murmur at this radius, and you want us to get two 200T cranes to do the same thing?" After a hurried whisper they

Alarm bells have stopped. Next, thread the coach between the cranes. *Dick Watson*

TAKING THE WEIGHT

said "Ok, we'll give it a go". Taking the weight again, both alarm bells rang this time, but they kept lifting and rapidly bringing the jibs up, the radius soon becoming less and so the bells stopped. I looked back at the drivers as the coach gently swung in the breeze, big smiles on their faces, they said "Easy mate, easy". Then followed the difficult task of manoeuvring the coach between the cranes, which was easier if I just kept an eye on it and left it to the crane driver's skill and experience, there was no point in me being a control freak if not needed. The coach was set down onto two nests of sleepers so we could do some basic hacking with a burning torch to make the centre pivots fit so that the bogies could be refitted for a trip to Heaton depot.

Whilst setting the coach down we came across another road crane bug. The coach was hanging on the cranes while the sleepers were adjusted, when without warning one end dropped suddenly by an inch or so, and everyone scattered. Asking the crane driver what had happened he said "Oh these cranes do that as the hydraulic oil cools" It happened several times, still unnerving even though we knew why.

While some of the Gateshead lads sorted the coach out so it could be put on its bogies, we turned our attention to the coach halfway down the bank, and the worst to pick up. Resetting the 160T crane to reach the far end whilst the 100T crane lifted two of the bogies on the track, we hoped to pick the coach up in one go and place it on the bogies in front of us so it could be moved away. Phil Crosby had arrived back on site just as we started to lift, and sure enough, as the cranes took the weight the 160T crane bell started to ring. "Why hasn't he stopped lifting?" asked Crosby, "Oh he knows what he's doing" I replied, getting the crane driver to jib up fast to reduce the radius while keeping the coach level, so the bell eventually stopped. "I hope you do!" said Crosby with a smile. The coach was soon in line with the track and a few bits had to be burnt off to allow the bogies to be refitted, with the now expected sudden drops from the cranes making staff scatter, even though we had sleepers in to catch the coach if required.

Dealing with the other coach part down the bank was a repeat performance, and this didn't take long. So we now had two coaches on the track, and they were manhandled out of the way so that we could recover two bogies from down the embankment to be fitted to the coach still behind us. The

L-R the two road crane drivers Jack Baldwin, Dick Watson, George Singh, Geoff Elliot,
Jack Wickham, Joe Glass (pouring tea), our train's secondman, Dave Lindsay,
Yours truly and Brian Porteous centre, with his back to camera.   BR

Gateshead team had made this coach fit to travel, so it was picked up and
threaded between the cranes and dropped onto the bogies without any
problems. Once this coach was ready, a loco and barrier wagon came and
took all three away to Heaton.

All that was needed then was one crane to re-rail the two rear coaches and
the power car, which, using a road crane didn't take long at all. We then
had to put everything away back in our tool vans, which took quite a while
as it was still a trek to the vans with all the packing and slings, though we
still had the Gateshead lads to help.

TAKING THE WEIGHT

It was noticeable that the MK3 coach bodies are very strong (as long as all the doors are closed!) and even the one that ended up on its side suffered no structural damage other than slight dents and scratches to the paintwork, hence no serious casualties amongst its occupants.

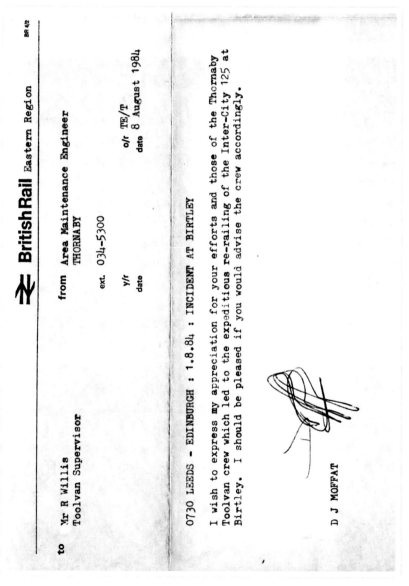

British Rail Eastern Region BR 4/2

from Area Maintenance Engineer
THORNABY

ext. 034-5300

y/r
date

o/r TE/T
date 8 August 1984

to Mr R Willis
Toolvan Supervisor

0730 LEEDS - EDINBURGH : 1.8.84 : INCIDENT AT BIRTLEY

I wish to express my appreciation for your efforts and those of the Thornaby Toolvan crew which led to the expeditious re-railing of the Inter-City 125 at Birtley. I should be pleased if you would advise the crew accordingly.

D J MOFFAT

Letter of Appreciation from the Depot Engineer for the way we quickly dealt with the HST derailed at Tyne Yard

The mess at Bedale. Tommy Armstrong looking at the tangle of wagons.   Dick Watson

TAKING THE WEIGHT

Bedale   2nd December 1988

A derailment at Bedale on the Wensleydale branch from Northallerton to Redmire on the 2nd December 1988 proved to be a bit painful for me. A rake of loaded lime wagons en-route to Redcar steelworks had become derailed just before the level crossing and made a mess of the single line trackwork. The level crossing was blocked by a wagon and we were required there as soon as possible to clear the road crossing, and as we didn't have a crane at that time off we went with the 'Bruff' and lorry.

On arrival it was obvious that it would take days to clear the line just by jacking, so I arranged for a road crane rep to come and discuss the options, but he couldn't come until the following morning. The wagon on the crossing was well derailed and it took some time to get it lifted up on four jacks, which were in turn mounted on trolleys on beams ready to be pushed across. (See photo of second wagon being re-railed) For some reason which I forget, when the wagon was nearly in line with the track it jammed, and I grabbed a push pull jack to give an extra bit of push, but the jack, when pushing, spat out of position and came back at me smacking me in the jaw. I can remember quite plainly doing a backwards somersault roll which my old PE teacher would have been proud of, (PE was a mystery to me at school and I consistently got the lowest mark he could give me (D-) at the end of term for my report) and landing on my feet to the loud applause of all the watching public bystanders!! So I just grabbed the jack and replaced it, and this time the wagon moved and we could then re-rail it.

The crossing was now clear, so the gates could be reopened for road traffic, but the next wagon was very close and we had to re-rail it. As time passed, my jaw started to ache like mad, but the job had to be done. Once that wagon was on the track there was nothing else we could do, so all the jacks were put away and we made ready for home. By then I didn't feel too good, so had the crew go back in the lorry and Dave Lindsay took me in the 'Bruff' to Northallerton hospital for a check up. There was no one in A & E, (not like these days!!) and a few Xrays later with a check over, the doctor just said "Take some painkillers, there's no damage, you're okay to go home". The following day I could hardly move and was black and blue with bruises all over my torso and legs, which seemed strange as I'd only been hit in the face, so Brian Porteuos, a relief Supervisor, dealt with the road crane and cleared the derailment up over the next couple of days.

The second wagon being re-railed showing the method of using MFD jacks.
Dick Watson

TAKING THE WEIGHT

Constable Burton   17th March 1989

Picking the first lime wagon up at Constable Burton. Dick Watson

A lime train from Redmire had come to grief while passing Constable Burton, and several wagons ended up in a heap. We hadn't got an official call as the Operating Supervisor on site wanted me to go and have a look first. This wasn't easy, going in my little van with an OS map, it took a few wrong turns down country lanes before I could find the level crossing I needed. (No Sat Navs then) The loco, with the majority of the wagons, was stood at the crossing, still waiting for me to do a simple brake test before it could carry on to Thornaby. The last wagon attached was derailed one pair of wheels, which we uncoupled and left. Walking up to the derailment proper, the track looked okay, but rounding a curve into a cutting the track just disappear into a tangled mass of rails and sleepers, with five wagons and the guards van all on their sides.

The P'way Supervisor was there with his boss, and it didn't take long to decide that they would have to open out the cutting and lay a new track in past the wagons a) because the line had to be re-opened as soon as possible and b) it would allow the crane to get alongside for recovery work to start. Walking past the wagons with the P'way Supervisor we could see that the wagons had derailed some distance back and looking at the marks on the rails it appeared that the track had cross level problems and possibly speed had been an influence, so Derby Technical Centre was called in to check everything and come up with a conclusion.

It didn't take long for the line to be re-opened, and a few weeks later we went up after the last Saturday train had cleared the line. I was training Tommy Armstrong at the time, so he came out with me and took a stint at supervising the crane, while I kept an eye on him. We also took a lot of spare bits of lime wagon, springs, horn guides, bolts etc. We knew that some wagons had lost their wheels and would need some work doing to make them fit to run. The tool vans had to have the crane marshalled at the end, so all the re-railed wagons could be pushed away from us as they were re-railed and collected by a loco to take to Northallerton for further repair. The job went easily enough, though it took time to find the wheels, put them on the track, then lift the wagon up, renew and repair whatever needed doing, then lower it onto its wheels. As they were loaded with lime, the load had obviously shifted, and some wagons when lifted didn't sit squarely. In one case it was so bad we had to slew the wagon to one side and drop the load through the bottom doors, then the wagon sat true in the slings so the wheels could be fitted.

Wondering where the wheels are!   Dick Watson

Uneven loading.

Dick Watson

TAKING THE WEIGHT

Snow and more snow

Depending on one's view point, snow was either the tool van man's friend or deadly foe. We got plenty of calls and overtime when it snowed, but working in snow could be dangerous and cold work. 1984 had some heavy snowfalls in January, and for several days we went from derailment to derailment, mainly caused by staff not clearing the snow out of points correctly in yards. It was difficult jacking in the snow, as things were wet, cold and slippery, so jobs took longer. A lot of time was spent just sitting in the vans waiting to get from place to place. Unless the derailment was stopping trains running, we were side-lined to let the operators struggle to keep them running under the difficult conditions. At one point we were out continually for four days, but suffice to say we had plenty of sleeping time!

The converted snowplough ADB9666509 stabled at Thornaby.   Terry Bye

A call came in for a snowplough derailed all wheels at Great Ayton on the Whitby branch. This was a converted 350hp shunting locomotive which had had its traction motors and side rods removed and air brakes fitted, along with a simple plough welded onto the front. The line was single track, and luckily for us it had been the trailing vehicle. The train crew had managed to uncouple it and continue down to Nunthorpe, which meant we could propel our train right up to the derailed plough. 350hp shunters are not the easiest of things to jack at the best of times, and the plough modifications made this one even worse to get hold of safely. The shunter's plough attachment had broken free, so the first thing was to use a jack to push it out of the way. Next job was to jack the vehicle up and sit it on steel plates so it could be pushed sideways to line up with the track. The snow wasn't too deep around the site, but even so it took four hours of hard work to re-rail it. Then we had to do some temporary repairs to the track ourselves in order to move the train up to get the crane nearer, then we could lift the detached snowplough up and place it on the jib runner.

It had been a lovely sunny day if bitterly cold, and we were all looking forward to getting back to the shed, unloading the snowplough and getting home. I had with me a Thornaby Supervisor, Peter Tuck who was learning the tool vans Supervisor's job. All day he had complained about the cold and now we were back in my compartment he was virtually hugging the gas fire. As we slowly went down the branch to Middlesbrough with the snowplough vehicle behind us, it was getting colder and colder and starting to snow heavily. We ground to a halt in Middlesbrough station and there was a tap on the window. The Station Supervisor was stood there with the snow whipping past him. A message from control, we had to go immediately to Etherley Tip, as a loco was trapped in the sidings by derailed wagons, and they were frightened that the loco would freeze up solid overnight. I explained we had to go to the shed to get rid of the vehicle and unload the snowplough first, and get coal and water for the crane, so begrudgingly they agreed - strange people in control at times.

With having to go to the depot, and the bad weather, it was past midnight before we arrived at Etherley. I was first out of the nice warm van, straight into a howling gale and heavy snow travelling horizontal to the ground, goodness knows what the temperature was, I'll just say there were no

The converted shunter snowplough before we started re-railing. L-R Anwar, Peter Tuck, Andy Findlay (Area Traffic Manager), Driver unknown, Joe Glass, Secondman unknown.

brass monkeys there! On finding the loco, there were two ballast wagons derailed in front of it, and the guards van derailed and buffer locked with the loco. I could get the crane next to the wagons thank goodness, as jacking would have been a nightmare in those conditions, but when Dave went on the crane he found all the pipes frozen so the injectors wouldn't work to put water in the boiler. His first job was to burn paraffin soaked waste rags to thaw the pipes out before he dare get the steam pressure up. The driver of the train had shut the loco down, so my first priority was to get it started before it froze as well. Cold class 37s don't like starting, but it did eventually, with lots of coughing and smoke from the exhaust. By that time Dave had got the boiler filled and steam up, but then he found the cylinders had frozen solid so he spent an hour in the driving snow gently working the pistons backwards and forwards and getting them warm until they ran freely. Then of course, all the shafts and gearing were frozen so they had to be worked until they ran free. In those conditions every one worked hard with a minimum of my telling them what to do, and given the horrific wind, snow and low temperatures, the wagons were re-railed quickly so we could get the crane put away and get back into the van for a hot soup. I asked the train crew to re-marshall the train with the cold class 37 coupled to our train loco, and put in multiple as well, so that the engine would be working to stop it freezing.

It took a long time to get back to the depot as signals and points were frozen and had to be sorted out before we could pass. Peter had to be put right next to the gas fire again with lots of hot tea so he could thaw out and get rid of his distinctly blue hue; Peter never went out with us again!!! We eventually got back to the shed at about 6 o'clock in the morning, and no sooner had I got home and into bed when the phone rang, another derailment at Darlington! Such was tool van life.

Battersby in the snow

There is a sharp curve in a shallow cutting just before entering Battersby Station from the Middlesbrough end of the branch, and drifting snow would always fill this cutting up given the chance. On 18th March 1979 two class 37s fitted with miniature snowploughs were constantly going backwards and forwards to keep it clear. Unbeknown to the operators, the railhead was slowly building up with a layer of ice, until one of the class 37s in the snowplough formation, 37212, came off one bogie on the ice. We propelled up to the derailed loco with the jacking van leading. The snow was halfway up the locomotive side by this time, so we had to walk along the top of the snow, then dig down to find the bogie and make enough room for us and the jacking gear. We had assumed that we were walking at the top of the cutting on snow that wasn't very deep, but we soon found out this wasn't the case in one area!!! Big John (Young) and Joe Glass were carrying a 120/60 ton jack between them, when all of a sudden Joe disappeared downwards with a 'plop'. Big John managed to keep hold of the jack, but looking for Joe all he could see was the top of his cap, and hear, muffled swearing. Where they were walking there was a cut-out in the embankment side which had filled with snow so it couldn't be seen, and even though we had all walked across it several times, it hadn't given way until Joe walked across it, which was surprising, as Joe was one of the lightest of the crew and Big John the heaviest. So we dug Joe out, which didn't take long, and once out he shook himself free of the snow, grabbed the jack with John again and carried on. Once the jacks were in position it didn't take long to lift the bogie, but it then took an eternity of difficult work to chip all the ice off the rails under the bogie before we could lower the wheels back onto the track. We removed the jacks to the side, and I got our train crew to start the locomotive up and slowly drive it back into Battersby Station. Once the loco was safely out of the cutting we could put the jacks away, as there was no point putting them away and then the loco coming off again. I told the P'way inspector that he would have to get all the ice chipped off the full length of track in the cutting before anything could run, and to keep an eye on it to make sure it didn't build up again.

A few days later we were back again! This time a DMU was off one bogie in more or less the same place, but we had the same amount of digging to do as the snow had blown in again. Getting down to the track it was obvious that the ice had built up, so much for discussing it with the P'way inspector. We soon had it back on the rails and this time I decided to move the DMU towards the tool vans so it wasn't trapped in Battersby until the cutting was made safe. We didn't get anymore calls to that location again, so the P'way had learnt their lesson until the thaw came.

Knowing when to say NO!

One thing one had to learn was to know when to say "No, I can't do that" or "I'll need assistance". It was all too easy to go and look at a derailment, say "We can do that", and once started realise you couldn't do it, or end up in dangerous situations. A case in point was a Class 31 that had come out of the Dinsdale Long Welded Rail Depot on 1st February 1987. For some reason the driver had gone past a signal at danger and the loco had gone through the catch point protecting the main line. The catch point had diverted the loco onto the embankment edge, and in the process it rolled over onto its side. Half an hour after the derailment I was asked to go and look at it and say what I needed to do the job.

Class 31 on its side at Dinsdale. Not sure what covering it with wagon sheets was meant to achieve.   Dick Watson

Getting there, the first thing I had to do was get to the loco, which was surrounded by the fire brigade scratching their heads. The officer in charge was rather abrupt, speaking to me as if I was the village idiot. Did I know how much fuel was in it, were the batteries isolated and such questions. Once he knew who I was and that I knew all about the loco, it just made him more unfriendly, so I ignored him. Not knowing what state the driver had left the loco (apart from being on its side of course) first job was to get inside and check everything was isolated; this was a problem as the cab door was now the roof and 12 feet in the air.

One of the fire brigade's lesser officers seemed a friendly sort, so I asked if he could get me up on top. No sooner said than a ladder appeared with a couple of firemen to assist me. Once on top I had to clamber into the cab where I hit my first problem. The cab door was hanging down and obstructing the door into the engine room, so the firemen lassoed the door handle and managed to lift it up while I squirmed into the engine room, hoping the door didn't drop, otherwise I'd be cut in half. Once in, I was stood on the electrical cubicle in the dark and feeling very disorientated, as things weren't where they should be. Very carefully I moved along until I got to the cupboard holding the main switch and lighting switch, which I turned off. Peering into where the engine was, I couldn't see it losing any oil or coolant, or any sign of a fire so I made my way back to the cab. The firemen hoisted me back out of the cab, and climbing down I was confronted once more by the same arrogant officer demanding to know what I'd done. I explained it was electrically safe now and wasn't going to burst into flames, and if a couple of his men could dig where I showed them, I would try to see what was happening to the fuel in the tanks. After a lot of digging I could see the tanks and the vents, which showed the fuel running out with little chance of us stopping it, so the firemen set up a bund wall around that part of the loco, and dug a hole for the fuel to run into from which it was pumped into barrels.

I knew my 45 ton crane wouldn't be able to do anything with it, and being situated on the edge of the embankment there was nowhere to place the jacks to turn it over, so I did a quick measure up, and looking at the 76 tonne crane capacity charts, figured out that two of them would be able to reach it, turn it upright then lift it. A quick phone call to Frankie Beattie at Gateshead had him on site within the hour weighing up what had to be done, as a JCB was needed to dig out to get ropes around the loco, and also organise Doncaster Crane, the job being set up to take place on the Saturday after the last train had gone. There wasn't anything Thornaby could do, so I got a lot of flak when I got back to the depot for us losing the job, but I knew we couldn't have done it.

I told Frank I would come along to watch and see how it went, but as luck would have it, while Gateshead were at Dinsdale, there was a derailment on the Saturday evening in their area which we had to go to, and I think we got more time out of that than if we had been at Dinsdale!

Fire Brigade

I'm probably being very unfair towards the Fire Brigade and their performance on the railway. I always remember the tale of a collision around the back of Middlesbrough station in 1963 where, in foggy weather, a class 25 Sulzer 2 ploughed into a guards van. The guards van had disintegrated and a pair of wheels landed in the cab of the loco, killing the secondman outright. The fire brigade arrived and wouldn't let any tool van man near it until they had recovered the body. Despite being told that the crane would lift the wheels straight out of the cab in minutes, they refused the offer and persisted in trying to cut the axle away, after several hours they gave up and the crane whisked the wheelset out in minutes and they could access the cab to do what they had to do.

A case in point with me was when a 45 ton tank wagon containing a dangerous highly flammable explosive chemical, derailed one pair of wheels in Tees Yard. All we needed to do was lift one end of the wagon up 6 inches, move it sideways 3 inches and it was back on the rails. Fifteen minutes to get the jacks out, five minutes to re-rail it and fifteen minutes to put the gear away. But I hadn't reckoned with the Fire Brigade officer!!! Any derailment of a tank wagon had to be reported to the emergency services, and this simple derailment warranted the attendance of four fire engines, an emergency tender, plus two police cars and an ambulance. The chief officer wouldn't let me go near the tank, let alone touch it, in case I triggered an explosion. I don't know what he expected it to do!!! It took the Op's manager, C&W examiner and myself nearly an hour to convince him that it would be safe to jack it up. His option to unload the tank where it was into road tankers would have been even more dangerous and taken days..

But before we could go near it he insisted that the fire engines were taken a ¼ of a mile away, hoses run from them to the tank and nozzles aimed at the tank. I asked him what they were for and he said "Oh just in case it explodes, then we turn the foam on!!" Five minutes later the tank had been re-railed, we put our gear away and had left, leaving some unhappy firemen to roll up miles of hoses. The tank wagon was examined, with no damage found, and on its way to Bristol an hour later.

Another day we were asked to provide a loco for the Fire Brigade so they could practice recovering bodies from the engine room and accessing the cabs. Having a collision damaged class 47 waiting to go to the works we offered them that. The loco was placed in a depot siding away from the depot and I and Geoff Tew, a fitter, stayed with it to advise as required. After a couple of dummies were placed in the engine room, a smoke canister was set off inside, and the firemen were sent in to recover the dummies, not an easy task in the limited clearances. When they came to access the cab I gave them the collision damaged end, knowing that the damage had jammed the cab doors. This had them flummoxed, being used to cutting cars open made from thin sheet steel, their cutting gear was too small to deal with the loco plate work, so they decided to smash the window, but loco cab front windows don't break! Attempts to smash the window to gain access to the cab proved futile as they hammered at it with an axe and then tried cutting it with a cutting disc. Seeing they weren't getting anywhere I asked Geoff to take the widow out, so taking a screwdriver he nipped up the front of the loco on a ladder, pulled the sealing strip out and with a twist of the screwdriver flicked the window out and onto the floor!!

Packing vans

When I took over the tool vans, all the vehicles in the train were in a bit of a state, i.e. ancient and past their best. They had all come with the 45 ton crane that was transferred from Darlington when the steam depot there closed in 1965. There was a riding van, which I have described earlier, an ex Gresley teak brake second, a converted wooden full brake of unknown origin, that housed the German light weight jacking gear, and lastly a MK1 full brake (BG) which was merrily rusting away as MK1 coaches do, this was used as the packing van, and carried all the wooden packing, chains etc.

The MK1 BG was condemned as unsafe in 1986, so a replacement was required. Historically, tool van vehicles have always been hand me downs from the passenger fleet, with slight modifications to make them fit for purpose, plus, the receiving depot would further modify the insides as required. The main alterations were to the riding vans, as bulkheads had to be removed and window and door openings altered. Of course the main depots, Gateshead, York etc. had modern immaculate vehicles as they were more in the public eye than us 'tuppence ha'penny' minor depots.

Steam crane ADRC 95222 in the snow at Thornaby. MK1 BG packing van furthest away and MFD van peeping into picture on the right. Early1985   Dick Watson

But back to the BG.. I had been given three months to get a replacement, but there were no spare BGs in the Eastern Region, and York therefore put me in touch with the London Midland region as they had spare packing vans. These were stored at Newton Heath, Manchester, and I duly went there to choose a van. On arrival I was taken and left at the far end of a siding where three vans stood rotting away. I chose the best one, as it had sliding doors - well they would once we repaired them! Amazingly, it only took three days for it to be checked over by the C&W Department at Newton Heath and arrive at Thornaby, which was very good going for BR.

The van, ADM 395478, was I think, originally Great Central in origin but heavily modified and had been fitted with gas lighting from some under slung gas bottles, but this system was damaged beyond repair. Enquiries confirmed that a normal coach electric lighting system couldn't be fitted - so what to do? More enquiries with the District Outside Maintenance Engineer (DOME) Supervisor on the depot, Maurice Graham, brought up that a set of batteries could be fitted and kept on charge whilst on the depot. It should be said at this time that strangely, all the equipment in the tool van, heating, lighting and the crane, were the responsibility of DOME. The snag was that the DOME staff was very busy, and it would be six months before this job could be done; I needed the job doing straight away so there was only one choice. Ten minutes later I was in the stores office ordering a set of class 37 batteries for a loco number that was on long term repair, and reels of wire and fittings. Suffice, the stores Supervisor was a pal of mine. Two days later I had all the material. Dave Lindsay was allowed to work with me for two days and Maurice said he wasn't bothered what I did.

Our brand new Jacking / Riding van, the MFD van peeps in on the right again. Dick Watson

Dave soon had the batteries in the van and was busy making a wooden box to house them. I was running wiring through the van and fixing the light fittings, when a head popped through the door with the fateful words "What do you think you're doing?" This was the DOME electrician and a union rep, who was said to be either left wing or a communist, depending on who you talked to. He wasn't bothered about DOME not being able to do the job in the time scale, or the tool vans not being able to go out and the consequences of that. No, it was their job, full stop. So, if I stopped what I was doing and removed everything, nothing else would be said, otherwise the tool vans would be blacked by the DOME staff. After a few seconds thought, I said to Dave "Pass that screwdriver so I can connect these wires". A knack of saying the right thing at the wrong time, or is it the other way round!!? So off he stormed, muttering threats under his breath.

The van was finished the next day, and with the help of extra bodies, all the packing and equipment swapped over. As you will have guessed, not having the DOME doing repairs or maintenance turned into a boon, as we did most of it ourselves, much quicker. The only problem looming was the crane's monthly exam which we couldn't do, but as I expected, the DOME fitters wanted the overtime and the crane was always looked after by them, blacked or not.

Down she comes

I can't remember which year, but it had been decided that the reinforced concrete coaling plant (coal cracker) used for steam loco's until the end of steam at Thornaby, should be pulled down. I use that term on purpose, as that's what we did!

The contractors given the job had to drop it within a certain area, and set about removing all the steelwork at the top and the wagon lift, and then they weakened the legs at the base. Now why they didn't use explosive charges I don't know, but I was called into the office, introduced to the contractor and asked to assist as necessary. The foreman in charge explained that he wanted to pull the cracker over in a certain direction, and that a loco would be ideal! So off I went to see the running foreman and arranged for a class 40 to be available the next day with a driver, and had a couple of tool van lads arranged to assist me.

Coaling plant with a WD 2-8-0 being coaled. Photo taken from the water tower.
John Cook

Came the day, and there was a window of an hour and a half when no loco's were going off the shed. The class 40 was sited on the outgoing road, and the contractors had fastened a long cable round the two nearer legs of the coal cracker. We used some of our tool van ropes to make up the final distance and hung them onto the class 40 coupling hook then we were ready. The affected area was cornered off and a British Transport policeman stood guard.... of what, I'm not sure.

The contractors wanted a slow steady pull, so I waved the driver to take up the slack and once the cables were tight to slowly throttle up. I was told the cracker was about falling down anyway and a little pull would do the trick, but no, the cables were twanging and no sign of any movement, so I went up to the driver and told him to give it the lot, and he pulled the power handle round to max, 2000hp, just sat there and eventually we got wheel spin. Abandoning that, I said we would sand the rails and gave it a slow running jerk; luckily the sands worked on the loco for a change and asking the driver to keep the sands on while we pulled once again, the cables went from slack to tight with a twang and there was a little sway on the cracker, but it still wouldn't come down.

The contractor said "Ok, we'll have to hack more off the legs and have another go tomorrow". Arranging the same situation for the following day wasn't easy, as loco's and crew aren't always spare, but with a bit of verbal pushing and shoving, I got what I wanted. Luckily, I had the same driver so he knew what was required, and repeating the slow steady pull from a slack to tight cable produced a definite sway on the cracker. I then signalled the driver to give it everything, and slowly the cracker heeled over and crashed down exactly where it was supposed to, with much applause from those stood watching, as the class 40 roared away down the line dragging the cable and a bit of leg behind it. Another one of those many unusual jobs that tool van Supervisors end up with.

Wheel lathe

Another strange job that came my way was when the Hegenscheidt Wheel Lathe was installed at the depot. This lathe was an under floor type where the loco, wagon or coach was driven over the lathe and the wheels could be turned in-situ without removal from the vehicle.

Contractors had spent weeks digging a large rectangular hole in No 6 road west pit, then lining the sides with concrete. Of course, they hadn't reckoned with the high water table at the shed, as the River Tees water level was just lower than the depot floor, so water seeped into the workings all the time, and then through the new concrete walls of the hole. Well, with all the fuel spillage over the years it was a mixture of diesel and water!! I can remember the pump they used to keep the workings dry failed one night, and when the contractors came the following morning, the hole was full to the top of mucky water. The final effort to stop the leaks was to pressure grout behind the walls, and finally they gave in and installed a pump in the deepest part of the hole where a swarf crusher would be located.

When the civil engineering works were finally handed over, two engineers from Hegenscheidt came over from Germany to install the lathe. This comprised two large heavy pieces that made up the lathe proper and lots of other bits. A small mobile crane was used to lift the pieces into the hole, and then I was asked to go and assist. The two parts of the lathe had to be set up in exactly the right place on the concrete beds prepared for them, so that the lathe was 100% accurate, I think the tolerance between each half of the lathe was 0.005mm. So using the 'Bruff' and small jacks we pushed the lathe around until the engineers were satisfied that it was somewhere near, and then height adjustments were required, which meant lifting the lathe very carefully while steel shims were fitted. Once that was done to their satisfaction, final careful movements got the two halves of the lathe set up against each other and the track to the required 0.005mm tolerance.

This of course didn't happen in a day, and it took nearly a full week to achieve the correct setting up - luckily we didn't get a call out during this time.

To drink or not to drink

In my early days on the tool vans things were a lot more lax on the railway regarding alcohol. There were usually a few bottles kept in the riding van, these being opened after a long job. I can remember a derailment on the main line near Durham where there were wagons everywhere, and Mr Reeves (Derek) was in overall charge of the job. Even though he was being pressurised to get the main line clear, he left it to me, and now and again would ask for an update. We worked hard all afternoon and into the night and by 10pm we were finished and the crane put away.

Mr Reeves had disappeared about 9pm as the last wagon was re-railed, and I thought he had gone home, but as we were getting washed and ready to leave the site there was a knock on the van side, usually the sign another derailment needing our attention. On opening the van door there was Mr Reeves and an operation manager, with two crates of beer for the 'lads' for all their hard work. Those were the days when staff was appreciated properly.

Tasks while not on the Tool vans

The period whilst I was tool van Supervisor was made even more interesting by all the varied jobs that came my way thanks to Jimmy Dean the Chief Maintenance Supervisor at the time, and later Phil Thickett. I'm not sure how or why, but my depot desk was located upstairs near Jimmy's office and next to his clerk Evelyn.

There had always been a divide between us scrubbers downstairs who got dirty, and the clerks. They were on a salary and got two more days holiday than us. So there I was sat with all the depot clerks, who eventually learnt to put up with me, I think. Jimmy Roberts, the chief clerk, certainly tried to make my life hell, but we eventually got on with each other.

Evelyn dashing back to her computer

Evelyn, being the technical clerk and working for Jimmy Dean, kept all the loco records up to date, filed all the examination and repair records in loco number order, and sent foreign (non Thornaby) loco records to the home depot. One of her main tasks was to work out the bonus for the maintenance staff every week. All the examination types and repeat tasks were coded by the Supervisors and had set times. Evelyn extracted these codes from the sheets, working out the bonus figure for the week from this information.

Of course, the workshop committee was never happy with the figure, and poor Evelyn had to plough through the figures all over again. Then of course there were times when the figure came out even lower, oh dear. As I sat near Evelyn, I was always being asked advice on codes and related items. Then in early 1980's the depot's first computer with MS. DOS arrived, which was for Evelyn's use to do bonus calculations, and also for storing a history of work done on any loco. The program used was called LOVERS (LOco VEhicle Record System). This had been developed in house at York, and an expert, Peter, was sent through to teach Evelyn how to use the computer and LOVERS. So of course, being there, I was able to be taught at the same time on this wondrous (well, then it was) machine, green screen and all. The program was unreliable to start with, so Evelyn had to run the manual system at the same time. Luckily the tool vans were quiet at the time so I was available to help keep LOVERS going for her. Eventually, the system was deemed reliable, the manual system was abandoned and her workload dropped off to a manageable level.

As to be expected, there was a continual running battle over the subject of bonus times, and one of the shop reps even managed to make it a full time job for quite a while, to check the figures produced by Evelyn. Of course he only managed to find the odd minute here and there, so the bonus figure for that week didn't change. I suppose in the eyes of the staff he was doing a good job and justifying his time spent looking at the figures, and from his point of view he didn't have to get his hands dirty. He did, of course, always manage to work every Sunday on the tools, as that was double time.

The staff were always complaining that the times for certain jobs were too tight, and eventually it came to a head with the time given for a turbocharger change on a class 47. Most times had been measured at Stratford TMD, and then imposed on all the other Eastern Region depots. The argument then was that each depot was different in the way its facilities were arranged, so times would be different. To resolve the problem at Thornaby it was decided to have the Work Study Department time a turbo change on a class 47. The next turbo change would have a dedicated fitter and mate allocated to it until it was completed; the shop reps then pulled a master stroke by insisting that Eddie McCluskey would be the fitter. Eddie was a very conscientious fitter, but a bit on the slow side with regard to how long it took him to do a job. Normally a turbo change took about a day, this one took a fortnight!! The staff was convinced that they would get a good time out of this.

The loco duly went back into traffic, and a week later the work study group came back with the results, and it turned out that Eddie had renewed the turbo in exactly the bonus time!! As the Work Study manager said, "All the time spent pondering on how to do it, or going back to get a tool or a joint from the stores, didn't count in the time, as the fitter should have taken them all with him when he started. The bonus time was based on actual work time not inefficient methods of working". After that it was rare to get a query on a bonus time from anyone.

I was always doing odd jobs, and these could be summarised as follows :- Overseeing and monitoring modifications to loco's; Fault finding on repeat faults; Trial runs; Quality control checks; Training; and many others..

Up and Over

Being experienced in dealing and making decisions about problems, I was usually called to deal with oddities. For example, one day my phone rang asking me to go and look at a class 47, 47052 which was stood on the goods line just next to the depot, so I didn't have far to go. The driver had reported a big bang, the loco had leapt into the air and then continued as if nothing had happened. Getting to the loco, the driver told me that he had been running along at 30mph and the loco had leapt into the air a foot or so with a loud bang, and then it had just run as normal. If this was true, then it would be obvious what had caused it. But no, I went round and round the leading bogie and found nothing. Eventually I finally twigged that the middle traction motor on the leading bogie wasn't in its correct place.

Traction motors are usually clamped to the axle on bearings so the gears stayed correctly meshed all the time, the other end being suspended by a link or spring arrangement to the bogie frame. In the case of the class 47 it is a link connected by a pin at each end. On 47052 the top pin had come out allowing the traction motor to drop down onto the track. It then jammed into a sleeper, the bogie lifted up and over, allowing the motor to pivot round further, and with its momentum it flew back up into the bogie frame and jammed solid against a stretcher. Thus it all looked normal when peering into the bogie with a torch, except of course the motor was the wrong side of that axle. By the way, traction motors weigh around 4 tons!!

Considering where the loco was in relation to the depot, and the motor hadn't dropped back down, even though driven a mile from its initial drop, I decided to chance having the loco driven to the depot. Telling the running foreman to supply another loco and driver, I helped the driver put handbrakes on and uncouple 47052 from its train. After isolating that traction motor, we slowly drove 47052 along the goods line to Thornaby station and then back into the depot.

The CM&EE at York were informed, and next day they sent an engineer to have a look and take photographs. Due to the position of the motor it wasn't safe to drop the wheelset out, so the loco was lifted off its bogies and the bogie placed under the drops crane. Once the crane was attached to the motor, it proved very difficult to get the motor to go down, and a small jack had to be used until it suddenly swung free. As the motor and wheelset had been subjected to severe forces, they were both renewed, along with a new link and pins, and away 47052 went back into traffic. As a result of this incident, a modification came out to fit brackets below the links to catch a motor if a pin came out. I would hate to think what would have happened if the motor had dropped when the loco was at speed and going in the other direction.

Class 37 fractured Bogie.

Being at Jimmy Dean's beck and call meant I got some oddball jobs, 37197 being a case in point. A Hartlepool driver rang up to say he had arrived at Cliff House sidings, and getting out of the cab had noticed that the bogie frame had a crack in it. Jimmy said "Let's go and have a look, I'm sure he's seeing things". On arrival, we found that No 2 bogie had fractured completely through the main box section of the bogie frame just behind the middle axle box horn gap. A complete check of the rest of the bogies showed no other obvious damage, so it was decided, after a conversation with control that a light engine move at 20mph to Doncaster works would be in order.

It took a day for the path to be arranged, and the next night I found myself at Hartlepool, sat in the trailing cab of 37197 above the fractured bogie, waiting for the last train to Middlesbrough to pass by. No sooner had the tail light disappeared than we got the signal, and we were off out of the siding onto the mainline. I had arranged with the driver that we would stop at Greatham then Stockton, Picton and Northallerton, while I looked around, and if anything went wrong I would slam the straight air brake on, my job being to monitor the bogie for problems and to make sure we didn't go above 20mph.

Now 20mph is slow, and we seemed to be getting nowhere fast, but every five minutes I would check the line side, and if there were no signals or bridges about I'd go down the footstep with my torch and peer at the fracture which had its two halves gently rubbing up and down. At Greatham I told the driver it was okay to go to Northallerton without stopping and I'd check there, so off we went again. By this time I was confident with the situation, and only went to look every ten minutes, and then every fifteen as nothing was changing. I knew if anything went wrong we would block the line from Teesside to Northallerton, and after that we were on the slow line all the way to York, so it didn't matter as much if we stopped. I'm sure control would have breathed a sigh of relief as we went onto the slow line; my check around at Northallerton hadn't shown any problems so I told the driver nonstop to York, at 20mph of course!! I only went down the steps to look once before York, and still everything was okay, so I was very confident now. As we left Northallerton along the slow line, several freights from Teesside rocketed by in quick succession, horns blowing at us for holding them up. As we approached York, I hoped the driver had remembered that I had asked for 5mph across all the pointwork, which would take us from the Up Slow across the River Ouse bridge then both fast lines and into Skelton yard. Of course he had, and we literally crawled a quarter of a mile into the yard. Any problem there and the whole of the East Coast main line would be blocked - no mobile phones in those days, just a signal man watching the track circuit lights on his panel as they changed from red to green as we progressed.

It had been arranged to have a half hour stop in Skelton yard, so I had a cup of tea with the driver. A final check of the bogie and off we went to stand at Holgate bridge signals waiting for permission to do the last leg of the journey. This last bit was very critical, as there were no slow lines or loops

37197 Bogie Fracture

to hide in as we left York until just before Doncaster, and we had a very slim path time to do it in as the mainline was busy, even in the early hours of the morning. As we entered the new section of track that bypassed the Selby coalfields, the ride improved a lot, so I went through to the front cab to be with the driver. He was worried that we would hold trains up, so I said "Take it up to 30mph as the new track is smoother here". Once we reached that speed I went back and peered at the crack - not a movement to be seen. So back to the driver, "Make it 35mph". "Are you sure about this?" he asked, "Absolutely" I replied, "On my head be it", and I stayed with him. Keeping to 35mph we soon approached the loop point, so I asked him to slow to 5 then back to 25 on the loop. Even though we had gone quicker, no sooner were we off the main line when a parcels train rushed by, horn blowing furiously, but looking at our schedule, we were ten minutes in front, so I'm not sure what he was complaining about.

I don't know if control had noticed our earlier arrival at the loop exit signal, but we then had to sit for over an hour while several trains passed before we were allowed onto the mainline and across into the works sidings. All the way through the journey I had been confident of getting to Doncaster without any hiccups, and so it proved. It had been a long night and we now had to wait for a train to Darlington, then to Thornaby, but luck was on our side. As we stood on the platform, an empty steel train came through, slowing down for the signal, and it was a Thornaby turn. The driver spotted us, and the train came to a grinding halt to give us a lift. That saved us a couple of hours and we got back to the shed at 9am, a long slow night, but they could be slower....

It goes without saying that on the modern (!) railway nothing like this, or a lot of what I am relating to in this book would be allowed, in any shape or form. They would be much happier spending days getting huge road cranes and road transporters involved, which equals £££££s, to achieve, with a lot of fuss, what we did in several hours as a matter of course, and no hold up to anyone.

Class 45 seized wheelset

A similar job awaited me a few months later when I had to keep an eye on a class 45 that had to travel from York depot to Thornaby to go on the drops. It had a seized traction motor bearing on a trailing wheelset of a bogie. As the bogies of classes 40 – 45 – 46 were too long and inflexible for a wheelskate to be fitted, the only way was to remove the leaf springs, fit packing below the axlebox so the wheelset rode high. Also, packing had to be fitted on top of the leaf spring of the next wheelset so the seized wheelset flange would ride higher than the rail top. York staff had done all this work and all I had to do was to turn up and ride it back to Thornaby.

Again, this meant travelling at slow speeds, in this case 15mph, and this to be strictly kept. As with 37197, the path had been arranged to ensure the minimum disruption to traffic. In this case we didn't have to go on the main line at all, and the only place not to stop would be from Northallerton to Thornaby. After the York driver had calmed down after being told it was 15mph all the way, (he didn't think he could go that slow with a class 45) I told him I had arranged with control and the signalmen that we would stop to examine the bogie at the north end of Skelton yard, Thirsk, Northallerton and Eaglescliffe, as I didn't want to be dodging trains on the main line.

At Skelton and Thirsk everything looked fine so on we crawled, but at Northallerton the packing on the leaf springs had started to move out. I had brought a quarter hammer just in case, and it came in useful in flogging the packing back into place. At Eaglescliffe, the situation was a lot worse, all the packing on one side had disappeared and the seized wheelset flange was now below rail level on that side. Decision time - what to do? I had a word with the driver and he was game for anything, so throwing caution to the wind I said "On we go". I told the signalman we would be crawling over every set of points with me watching the wheel until we got to Thornaby, and after a minute's thought he said "Okay lad, but we won't be telling control will we?!" Well we didn't want them to know because I'm sure they would have stopped us, but if they found out, too late. "Oh, and you have 35 minutes to get to the shed before the next train's due" he added.

We slowly crawled down towards Bowesfield junction with all its points, and my heart was in my mouth as the wheelset squealed and bumped its way over all those point blades and crossings. The driver watched me like a hawk as I walked alongside the bogie, ready to slam the brakes on at my signal. At last we reached the entrance to the depot, and as the bogie cleared the main line, there was a loud bang as the rest of the packing shot out and the wheelset dropped down. A close call indeed! I told the driver to carry on and just drag the wheelset along, as it didn't matter in the depot.

Six months later I had to do the same with a class 40 from York, but this time I insisted the packing was all welded together and fitted with nibbs to stop it moving about. Consequently, I arrived at Thornaby without any problems and all the packing in place…

Plates and more plates

Another small task I had was nameplates for the official naming of loco's, drawings would be sent from Doncaster drawing office showing the exact location they should be on the loco side, which I found wasn't always suitable, due to the location of body frameworks or conduits, so artistic licence in positioning was used a few times!! I think I fitted the majority of nameplates at Thornaby, including driving every time to the makers at Nottingham to collect them.

47363 named 'Billingham Enterprise' at Darlington station 6th December 1985.
Shows the attention to detail usually given at these events, the pelmet with curtains closed

TAKING THE WEIGHT

The plates came pre drilled for fastening holes and 'Advel' rivets were used to hold them securely in place. These rivets were, I was told, used to fasten aircraft together as they could be fitted into a hole through two items from one side only, then, using a special tool, the rivet could be tightened up until its stem broke off at a pre-determined torque, leaving the rivet head flush. The other thing was that these rivets were extremely difficult to remove, so the plates couldn't be stolen unless you had a very good electric drill and special drill bits.

L-R Yours truly, Unknown, Richard Peck (Depot Engineer)
The five 37s stretch behind us with 37062 directly behind us. 30th September 1985
Phil Thickett

Every time we named a loco it was brought in a few days before the naming day, given a thorough clean and paintwork touch up if required, the buffers were cleaned and scrubbed then painted white along with the tyre sides. Loco's done this way just sparkled, and every depot was proud of the finish they could achieve in bulling loco's up. Once the plates were fitted, a black plastic bag was taped over them so the perennial train spotters that were about couldn't get a photo before the ceremony. The next thing was to fit screws to the body above both plates to hang a curtain pelmet on level and securely, and very important, check that the curtains would open every time!! Wherever the loco was to be named, I followed along with the pelmet for the official to open via the usual cord system, after they had said suitable words for the occasion of course. My position was by the side of the pelmet just in case a helping hand was required!

I think the highlight of these occasions was when we named five 37s all at the same time on the depot. These loco's were all named after British Steel locations and would be used in pairs on a very important train that ran every day from Lackenby to Corby in Northamptonshire, carrying coil. The problem was making sure we had enough pelmets for them all, and a mayday was sent to all depots for a loan of their curtains!!

All five 37s sparkling in the sun   Phil Thickett

The Demons arrive

Another part of my duties was being seconded to help the Derby Technical Centre fit two class 37s with what was then high tech equipment to monitor the loco's. This was code named 'DEMON' Diesel Electric Monitoring. Alan Hirton was the scientist involved, and he and his assistants (Bob ?? and Kevin Fry) made several visits to the depot to fit out 37512. Thornaby was chosen because our 37s worked very heavy steel trains for long distances ie the Corby trains.

The work involved was to fit sensors to as many parts of the loco as possible ie turbo speeds, fuel pressures, water temperature at several points, camshaft rotation alternator voltages, traction motor voltages etc. etc. Alan had sourced, or made, sensors to suit each application, and this meant lots of cables running back to a box mounted in the clean air compartment which held a computer. The final touch was a modem coupled to a mobile phone, which meant Alan could ring the loco up from his office and monitor anything, or download a day's worth of data. As I said, old hat now, but cutting edge then. My part was to advise where cables could run, or how to fit things so they didn't get in the way, but of course I got stuck in when I could help. Once the work was completed, Alan took a long time calibrating all the sensors, and it turned out that the phone link wasn't easy to set up and keep working reliably, so I would get a phone call asking me to download the computer onto a floppy disc (remember them?).

Phil Thickett was one for doing things off his own bat and promoting the depot. He came up with the idea to name 37512, the obvious name being Thornaby Demon. So plates were ordered and duly fitted, Alan doing the honours.

As 37512 was a success, it was decided to fit another loco and 37506 was chosen. This time all the work would be done at the Tech Centre, so still being seconded to the project, I went for a week to Derby to assist. The Tech Centre was several worlds away from the depot, it was a pleasure working there knowing that the stores had everything one would ever need, and it was clean and warm. I spent all week fitting conduits and running cables, and all Alan had to do was follow on fitting his sensors and computer. I was well looked after whilst there, being put up in the Midland

Hotel opposite the station (4 star treatment), and one of the lads would take me out somewhere on an evening.

A different system of communication was used on this one which was certainly more reliable. 37506 was already named British Steel Skinningrove, so there was no need for a special nameplate.

Once the two loco's were up and running, whenever possible they were put on our heaviest jobs, usually a Corby turn. If these loco's developed a fault we could ring Alan and he would ring(!) the loco up and look at the readings, pointing us in the right direction. He could tell us for instance, whether oil, fuel or air filters were blocked, or if there was a coolant temperature problem, and lots more.

Unauthorised modifications (Mod's)

When Phil Thickett arrived as Chief Maintenance Supervisor, he had a more liberal view of York CM&EE, BR, and official dictates, as I shall relate.

Thornaby had a diagram for a class 31 that meant the loco was away from the depot for several days, and usually arrived back with the fuel tank empty if not failing due to being out of fuel. So Phil asked if I could look into modifying a class 31 to utilise the old boiler water tank as a fuel tank. At this time there were a couple of the older fitters on light duties, Dave Ruddick and Geoff Hopper, so it was easy to get them to help me when required.

Not all the class 31s still had boiler water tanks, so it was a case of selecting one that wasn't long out of works with the water tank in good condition. I think 31178 was chosen. I spent some time figuring out what to do as the water tank was up in the body while the main fuel tank was below, between the bogies, giving a big height difference between the two. Dave and Geoff helped by saying whether something could be possible or not, and eventually I had some drawings ready. Basically we had to make the main fuel tank completely tight with a vent pipe going up into the loco body (the end being higher than the top of the water tank), wash the water tank out thoroughly to remove rust etc. fit a gauge and a fuel connection instead of the water connection, and finally a pipe to connect it to the main fuel tank.

L-R   Kevin Fry, Bob ??, Alan Hirton, Yours truly, and John Atkinson

TAKING THE WEIGHT

When the chosen loco came in for a major exam we set to, and after a couple of days it was completed. It had been a bit of a fiddle getting some of the pipework in but Dave and Geoff managed. We had increased the capacity from 650 gall to about 800 gall, so off the loco went into traffic, and the running side were asked to use the loco on that specific job where every drop of fuel counted. After a few weeks, Phil had a phone call asking why there had been no more failures on this train due to fuel shortage. I don't know what Phil said, but it kept them happy, and 31178 stayed in this condition for years, though I think the extra tank ceased to be used when it wasn't required.

Another problem Phil wanted to address was loco failures with flat batteries, usually due to lights being left on or the BIS (Battery Isolation Switch) being left in. Enter stage left Brian Cheetham, an electrician. We often worked together on electrical faults and talk was often about how to stop flat batteries. So when we had a feasible plan, off we went to Phil who said "Go ahead".

A class 31 was the easiest to modify as all the wiring came to a central point in the control cubicle with fairly easy access. 31281 was the chosen loco, as again it was on major repairs and in for a few weeks. It wasn't that easy to find room in the cubicle for a couple of extra relays and a contactor, so the job took longer than we thought.

The day eventually came when we switched the lights on, and 30 minutes later out they went. A notice had to be put in the cabs saying that if the engine wasn't running, all the lights except the tail and marker lights would go out after 30 minutes, and to reset, the main lighting switch had to be switched off and back on. Locally this was considered a success so another loco 31282 was modified in the same way.

The problem with 31178 – 31281 – 31282 was that eventually they would go into the main works for overhaul. Then all hell would break loose, unauthorised modifications were just not allowed, no matter how good they were. So when each went into the works, the phones would ring, nasty letters would be written, and how Phil dealt with all that I don't know, but nothing ever came of it all. When 31282 came back from works it was back to standard but 31178 and 31281 each seemed to survive a couple of works visits, coming back as we had modified them.

Official modifications

There were a lot of official mods on the go in the 1980's and I was the man looking after them all. This involved getting the instructions, and ordering the drawings and material to suit the number of loco's allocated. Once the material arrived, I had to sort it out, check quantities, and make them into kits for a loco.

As the number of mods on the go at once built up, I managed to get hold of a condemned 2 axle parcel van and had it placed in the roundhouse. Unlike the saga with the tool van packing van, this had a working set of lights and batteries, and all I had to do was rig up a battery charger. There was a lot of spare racking in the stores, so having acquired that and a couple of spare fitter's mates for a day, the van was all set up and all the mod material could easily be stored away until required.

Once we had the drawings and the material, the next task was to figure out how the mod was to be done. You didn't get many instructions or guidance, except there was already a bonus time!! Then I would allocate the loco when it was in for either an exam or repair, and go on with the staff to see the first mod of that type to be done then monitor its progress until finished and tested if required. All that was left to do then was complete the paperwork and send it off to York for their records.

Mod's that come to mind of the many that we did are-

1) Class 37 electromagnetic fan clutches to stop cool running

2) Alterations to class 20 & 31 cooling system pipework to bleed warm water to the radiators in winter.

3) Converting water tanks on class 37s to be fuel tanks

4) Fitting spark guards above wheelsets on class 47s

5) Fitting national radio plan wireless telephones to all classes.

6) Rebuilding class 08 cabs to be better insulated and fitting an electric heater.

7) Fitting guards around the turbocharger on class 47s in case they exploded!

At the time, York CM&EE had two engineers who looked after mods on the Eastern region, Dave Wragg and Vernon Broadhead. On large mod's they would go around the depots to see how things were going and check the first two that we did. They were also available to sort out any problems that arose, mainly because what the drawing office thought, didn't actually work out in practice.

The Class 37 Fan Clutch mod was a case in point. As built, the class 37s had a direct drive from the engine auxiliary gearbox through a right angle gearbox and up to a centrifugal clutch which drove the roof mounted fan, thus drawing air through the radiators. Over the years it became apparent that this system could lead to over cooling of the engine, leading to oil lacquering on moving parts and causing problems. The solution was to replace the centrifugal clutch with an electro-magnetic one; this was energised when the coolant temperature rose to a certain level, and dropped out when the temperature came back down. It was found that when ticking over the clutch very rarely came in, thus keeping the engine warm. March depot had done the first ones, so Vernon took me with him to March to look at one, get advice and see how they did it. On the way home, looking at my notes and the drawings, I thought I'm sure it could be done easier than this. So after we had done two as per the drawing, the two electricians involved, Keith Coates and Rob Bateman, came to me and said there are easier ways to do this by re-siting the control box and conduit runs, and it would be quicker. So I contacted Dave Wragg and explained what we thought. He wasn't keen at all on any changes, but eventually relented and said we could do one to our design, and then he would come and look. Dave came along after our re-designed mod was completed and was pleased. As well as being quicker to do it also used less material and looked better. So he took photographs and measurements, and the drawings were altered so all the remaining loco's were done our way!!

The class 37 fuel tank mod was brought in to enable the loco's to do longer diagrams without re-fuelling. It utilised the ex-boiler water tank, which is situated next to the fuel tank between the bogies. On paper this was a simple mod to do. All that was needed was a flexible connection between the tanks. The main works were going to do the mod, but there was a need for it to be completed in a shorter timescale, so Thornaby was chosen to do some.

Having got the drawings and material to do five loco's, I had a word with Jimmy Dean and had a loco that was on repairs donate a water tank for us to modify, and then we would always have a spare tank being worked on. 37100 was the loco, and any train spotters among you will remember this loco looking odd with the tank missing (I'm not sure if a model was produced by one of the OO model firms in this state).

The first thing was to see if we could get the tanks down on the drops. According to the measurements they should, but would they?? After figuring out how the tanks were fastened in place, we put the small trolley we used for removing wheelsets on the drop table with a bit of wood packing, went up to the tank, took the weight and removed the bolts. Gingerly lowering the tank, we had 6 inches to spare all round and then a bit of a jiggle to lift it up out of the drop hole onto the floor.

I had appropriated a modern P'way trolley for the tank to sit on while we modified it and the first job was to remove all the access doors and fittings that had suited its use as a water tank. Peering inside, I wasn't sure what to expect, as these tanks had carried water then been left to rot away over many years, and now it had to carry 600 galls of fuel, safely. Luckily this one was in fairly good condition, and it was pushed on the trolley from 4 road into the shunting shed 3 road, where the bogie cleaning equipment was. Several shifts were then spent washing out the tank so that it was spotlessly clean inside, all sludge and scale removed.

As we did more loco's we came across tanks that had rotted away that much we had to send them to Doncaster for repair, so we pinched another loco's water tank, to provide a spare to work on, and when we got the tank back from Doncaster that loco was next in for the mod. The good thing about sending the tank to Doncaster was that it came back as new, painted fully inside with all the fittings blanked off, and the pad for the flex pipe already fitted.

Once the tank was clean inside, another inspection took place to check for wasting of the tank, and that the anti–surge baffles were in place and not rotted away. Joe Glass, the boiler smith, did all the depot welding and plate work etc. He was seconded to me to do all the work on the tanks, apart from removing and re-fitting them. After I had marked out on the tank the position where the pad had to be welded, he burnt a hole and welded the pad in place. The old water tank overflow pipe was removed, and a new one fitted which had a couple of bends in it so that the top 'U' bend was level with the top of the tank, well above the full point of the fuel, as we didn't want a full tank of fuel being able to slop onto the floor when the loco was moving. Finally it was given a coat of red oxide and then black paint, and we had a fuel tank.

The first loco chosen came in, the fuel tank drained and then sited on the drops. I marked out the positioning for the pad to be welded, and the water tank was dropped out for cleaning and conversion. The loco then had to go into No 3 road for the fuel tank to be washed out, a steam nozzle being left in for 24hrs to ensure there was no fuel or fumes left. We didn't want to be burning a hole in the tank for it to go bang!! A scientist came from the Tech Labs at Doncaster to check for fumes with a gadget on the first two, but he went away happy, (We never got a bang, pop or even a fizzle on any of the tanks we did, but you couldn't get away with doing this today). I was quite certain that we could have burnt and welded the tanks without cleaning, but I wasn't allowed to try.

Once the tank was deemed safe (!), Joe then burnt a hole in it, welded the pad in place, and we were ready to go. The tank was replaced, the 3 inch bore flex hose fitted, and off to the fuel point to see what happened. Bit of an anti-climax really. The loco took twice as long to fill obviously, with not a leak anywhere, thank goodness. Though it wasn't noted on the drawings, I had the loco's work in our area for several weeks, and at every 'A' exam the fuel strainer would be cleaned and the fuel filter renewed to make sure that they weren't clogging with debris from the water tank, which going by the condition of the strainers on the first A exam was a good idea.

The job became a routine easy task, and it was planned that we did one a week, as long as the drops weren't needed for wheelset changes. Then disaster struck. I got a phone call to say a double tank loco being fuelled had overflowed because the auto shut off valve (Flyte Valve) hadn't worked, and it was now pouring fuel into the pit. When I got there, there was a solid stream of fuel coming from the overflow pipe, which showed no sign of stopping. After a moment's panic, I said we would have to let air into the top of the tank, and luckily there was a small blanked off pipe we could remove the blank from. As soon as the blank was removed, there was a rush of air into the tank and the flow stopped. We reckoned that we had lost about 700 gall of fuel into the drains, so the next rush was to the interceptor to see what was happening. Luckily, the system, though working overtime, coped with the sudden rush of fuel and not one drop got to the River Tees. I had the loco sited on a pit, clambered as far as I could up the end of the tank, and reached up with my fingers to the top of the 'U' bend on the vent pipe, and no hole. A ¼ inch hole was supposed to be drilled in the top of the 'U' bend to break any syphon effect that might occur during a overflow. The only silver lining was that this loco had been modified in the works a few weeks previously.

The only way I could see to get the hole drilled was to drain the tanks and drop the tank down on the drops. The drops were busy at the time so the loco would have to stand a few days, which would have caused questions from on high. As I stood by the loco, 'Black Jack', Jack Forster came by, laughing at me and my problem. Ten minutes later he was back with a ladder and an electric drill. Going into the pit and sticking the ladder up the side of the tank, he disappeared up it. After ten minutes of severe swearing and cussing, the drill could be heard running, and after 5 more minutes of swearing and drilling, he re-appeared even more filthy black than before, sauntered off, hole drilled. I could just to say get my finger to where the hole was, let alone a drill, so how he did that I'll never know. Black Jack was an ex steam fitter whose skills meant no job was impossible to him, though swearing loudly all the time was an essential ingredient. At the end of the day he had got a loco into traffic and the strange thing is if I'd asked him to do it he wouldn't have, well not straight away!!

Shunter Cab Mod

As built, the 350hp shunters, now designated class 08, were very basic when it came to the interior of the cabs. Though a huge improvement from steam loco's, once the more modern diesel loco's came along there would be lots of complaints from the drivers about being cold or sitting in drafts. The cab was essentially a steel box, with either wooden or aluminium cab doors. There was no insulation on the steel plates, and all the conduits and air pipes etc. were just clipped to the steelwork. There were three small finned water radiators, one under each cab seat and one under the electric cooker. The radiator water was from the engine coolant system, so on a cold morning the engine had to warm up before any heat could be felt in the radiators, not that they really did anything even when hot. This meant, in desperation, the cooker would be put and left on, but it not being designed for continuous operation, of course would eventually burn out. The front and back windows were glass in a steel frame which could be opened for cleaning or wiper repairs. Of course the steel frames warped over time and didn't fit in the body properly so were always found stuffed with paper in an attempt to keep the drafts out.

In the 1980's the unions' complaints about these loco's must have eventually got through to the BR top managers, and a program was instituted to modify the cabs. This was a big mod that should really have been done in main works, but as it was now rare for these loco's to go to works, certain depots were chosen to do the mod. At first Thornaby wasn't one of them. Sheffield Darnell was the nearest as they were a large wagon depot with a declining workload so had plenty of staff available. However, the number of loco's being done wasn't fast enough, so Thornaby was asked to do some. Being the 'Mod Man' I was asked to see if it was feasible, so I went over to Darnell to see what was involved and how they managed it. Vince Broadhead was the York engineer overseeing the Eastern region loco's and he came along to tell me all about it. I took a camera and loads of photos and asked questions of the staff.

The mod was quite big, it required the cab stripping out as much as possible, spacers welded in to support existing equipment, conduit and air pipes away from the steel cab platework. The old water heater pipework had to be removed and blanked off, the cooker thrown away, and alterations were needed to the console. Then a framework was welded into place to hold pre-cut sheets of 'Formica' over insulation, which was clamped in by aluminium strips. Then the air pipes and conduit were refitted, along with a new combined heater cooker unit. The heater wasn't that high an output, but at least had a fan to blow the warm air around. The auxiliary electrical supply wasn't designed for a high load so there was a switch to select either heater or cooker.

The alterations to the control cubicle meant that the straight airbrake handle had to be shortened. As the loco could be driven from either side,

08582 after its cab modification and repaint   Dick Watson

TAKING THE WEIGHT

the air valve was operated by a long shaft with a handle at each side. This shaft needed altering, so the actual handles were shortened, and one was moved along the shaft by 8 inches. This was beyond our ability as the shaft needed a keyway cutting in it. I approached several local machining firms, but they didn't seem to be interested in a small job like this, or on an infrequent basis. I was getting a bit stuck with this aspect, until someone said why not try the main DOME workshop at Gateshead. A few phone calls later, and I was off to Gateshead with a drawing of the alterations needed.

The DOME shop was situated in the building that had originally been the main locomotive works of the North Eastern Railway until Darlington Works opened in 1863 (Gateshead works then doing heavy overhauls until 1959). The shop had a good selection of machines, which of course the DOME department would need access to as they did a lot of different jobs. The discussion with the Supervisor there was fruitful, and he didn't see a problem doing the work on the shafts, but he would only do them as and when he had spare capacity. To get over this I arranged to rob shafts off some scrap 08s we had and send them to him; this would give me a float.

There only remained the question of who would actually do the work, and a bit of negotiation meant I could have Steve Carr and Andy Lambert on a long term basis. This was excellent, as both of them were good all-rounders who could put their hands to anything. York had decided which loco's they wanted us to modify, and 08582 was the first in and also due an 'E' exam, so I ordered two kits of parts which arrived shortly afterwards. It was a long job sorting through all the parts against the drawings, and in some cases, puzzling what on earth a particular bit was, and they were placed in the mod van in order of being needed, or what we thought the order was.

08582 came into the bottom of 3 road after its 'E' exam and Steve and Andy set to stripping the cab out and removing the water heaters. These heaters and their pipework were a nightmare, as they had been in place for 20 to 30 years and were either rusted solid at the joints or rotten, so new pieces had to be fitted to keep the coolant system leak free once the blanks were fitted. The mod wasn't straight forward, but having Steve and Andy meant that in most cases they sorted any problems out as they went along. 08582 took a long time to complete, which was to be expected being the first one we had done, and a lot of lessons learnt on the way. An advantage of this mod was that we could buy anything that would make the job easier, so all sorts of tools and special drills etc. were obtained on the mods budget.The finishing touch was Steve's idea, to have an etched plastic plate placed in the cab that said '08582 cab modified at Thornaby TMD'.

As always, as the mods progressed Steve and Andy found better ways to do things, or even alter the mod to make something easier or better, but this time we kept quiet about it and just did it. Every loco was inspected by Vince Broadhead before release, and he was well pleased with the standard of work and finish in all the loco's Steve and Andy did. The drivers appreciated the cabs in the winter, as they were definitely warmer. In some cases if they didn't get a modified cab loco for their shift they would go and see if they could swap for one, but the combined heater cookers weren't reliable and caused problems all the time.

In conclusion...

There you have it, a brief resume of my early railway days and tool van experiences as I remember them. Whilst writing, it has brought back long forgotten memories of happy, though occasionally hard times.

This book stops at the end of my tool van years, but if pushed, I could maybe start writing again of my final years, but I'll let the reader decide that!

I appreciate that there will be lots of gaps in what I have written as I often thought as I neared the end of this book, "I should have written about this, or that", but space and time precludes adding them, and again, maybe a Book Two would include them.

Looking back I wouldn't have changed anything and thanks must go to Mr Clothier who set me on the right track!!

List of all the bridges Thornaby renewed

Date	Place
?/77	Northallerton Bridge
?/?/78	Thirsk bridge
27/1/79	Ryhope
12/5/79	Ryhope
19/5/79	Ryhope
27/9/80	Port Clarence
1/11/80	Port Clarence
29/11/80	Tursdale
6/12/80	Tursdale
13/12/80	Tursdale
12/4/81)	Stannington
16/5/81	Darlington South
20/6/81	Darlington South
25/7/81	Darlington Ketton
10/10/82	Brompton
17/10/82	Brompton
12/12/82	Bridlington station
18/12/82	Bridlington station
6/3/83	Northallerton station
19/3/83	Bridlington station
2/4/83	Bridlington station
9/4/83	Bridlington station
12/5/84	East Cowton
19/5/84	East Cowton

whilst I was in charge

Details

B6271 bridge

B1448 bridge

Bridge 243 cancelled - adverse weather

Bridge 243

Bridge 243 completed

Renew bridge No 9

Renew bridge No 9

Renew bridge 169 Up Line

Renew bridge 169 Down Line

Completing bridge 169

Rebuild bridge 65 (civil eng crane had failed)

Renew bridge 98 Smithfield road

Complete bridge 98

Renew parapets on viaduct, bridge 110

Renew bridge 119

Renew bridge 119

Renew bridge 19

Renew bridge 19

Renew underbridge No 57 (middle of platforms)

Renew bridge 19

Renew bridge 19

Renew bridge 19

Bridge 76 renewal

Bridge 76 renewal

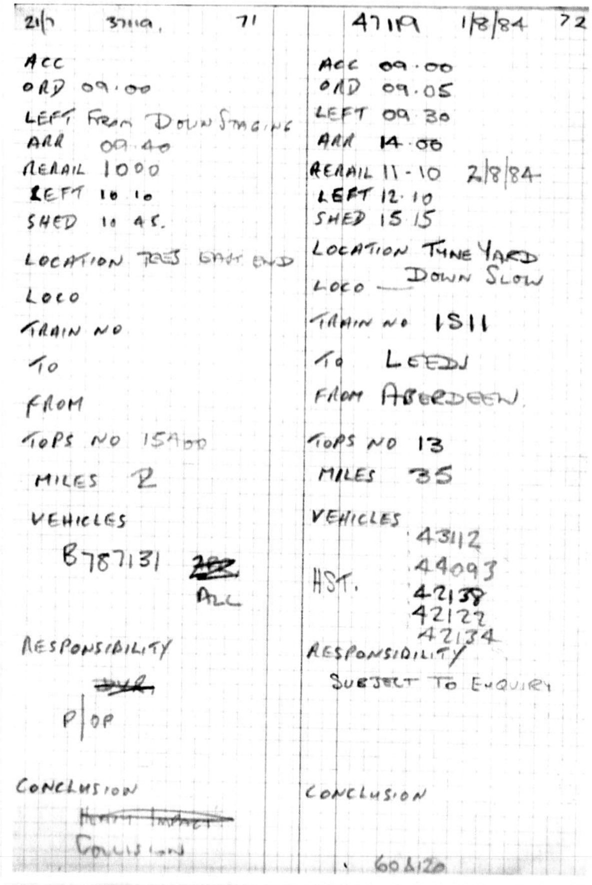

21/7   37119,   71

ACC
ORD 09.00
LEFT From Down Staging
ARR 09.40
RERAIL 1000
LEFT 10.10
SHED 10.45.

LOCATION ?? EAST END

LOCO

TRAIN NO

TO

FROM

TOPS NO 15900

MILES R

VEHICLES

B787131 ~~282~~
                  ALL

RESPONSIBILITY

~~YR~~
P/OP

CONCLUSION
~~Heavy Impact~~
Collision

47119   1/8/84   72

ACC 09.00
ORD 09.05
LEFT 09.30
ARR 14.00
RERAIL 11.10   2/8/84
LEFT 12.10
SHED 15.15

LOCATION TYNE YARD
          DOWN SLOW

LOCO

TRAIN NO 1S11

TO LEEDS

FROM ABERDEEN

TOPS NO 13

MILES 35

VEHICLES
          43112
          44093
HST.   42158
          42122
          42134

RESPONSIBILITY
   SUBJECT TO ENQUIRY

CONCLUSION

   60 & 120

Example of Derailment Logbook

The scan opposite shows two entries in the log book for 1984. These books were whatever I could scrounge from the stationery cupboard, and as they were kept in my desk, then taken to the job, they had a rough life and some fell to pieces well before the year was out. I have managed to keep hold of most of them (1979 1980 1981 1982 1983 1984 1985 1986) and they're now safe with me at home.

The right hand entry is for the HST derailment mentioned in this book. Obviously, there is a date, along with the entry number for 1985, in this case 71 and 72. At the top is the date and loco number used to haul the Tool vans (37119 or 47119). If the 'Bruff' was used then it would say 'Road'. The left hand entry vehicle has 'All' next to it, meaning derailed all wheels. The rest of the page is, I hope, self-explanatory.

The book was usually entrusted to a Tool van member to get the basic details while I weighed up the job, and I would fill any missing details in before leaving. On return to the shed I transferred all this information onto a form. These forms were done in duplicate (using carbon paper!), one copy going off to the Newcastle Engineering offices, where clerks entered the details from all the sheds in the region onto bigger forms, so that trends could be determined. The other form was kept by me in the shed record system.

Number of calls attended

1977	393
1978	Book missing
1979	225
1980	140
1981	132
1982	100
1983	120
1984	97
1985	80
1986	80
1987	41
1988	58

The steady decline in calls per year can be seen as older derailment prone wagons were replaced and yards and sidings were closed, as the majority of derailments occurred in them.

Vehicles used in the Tool vans 1970 to 1990

ADM 395478   Replacement packing van from Newton Heath?

ADE 975055   MFD van (converted Thompson LNER full brake)

ADB 975476   Mess / jacking van (converted MK1 BSK)

ADE 321112   Old riding van (ex Gresley LNER Brake Second Coach)

ADB 977099   Old packing van (ex BR MK1 full brake)

ADRC 95217   45 ton capacity built by Cowans and Sheldon of Carlisle
              (ex Darlington)

ADRC 95222   45 ton capacity built by Cowans and Sheldon of Carlisle
              (ex Finsbury Park)

ADRC 96700   75 ton capacity built by Cowans and Sheldon of Carlisle
              (ex Gateshead)

If the allocated crane went for overhaul or repair, we had through our hands
various other cranes. The ex Cambridge 45T crane 330133, & Healy Mills
45T 330107 come to mind.

On receiving the Tool vans complete from Gateshead we then had

ADB 975482   MFD Van

ADB 975463   Riding Van

ADB 975498   Generator Van.

Glossary of Terms

Backhead – the back of the boiler on which was mounted water gauges the firehole door etc.

Boilersmith – a time served tradesman who looked after steam loco boilers. They were also trained in gas burning / welding and electric welding.

Buffer Beam - end of the loco or wagon on which were mounted the buffers, air cocks for the brake system and electrical cables between locos

Bund wall – a barrier put around an area that contains dangerous fuel or chemicals to contain them.

Catch point – A set of points designed to deflect a train that has passed a signal at danger away from a running line.

Clack Valve – a valve that only allowed water to go one way through a pipe into the boiler against the steam pressure.

CM&EE – Chief Mechanical and Electrical Engineers department. Where the top engineers worked for the Eastern Region. Based in Hudson House York.

C&W – Carriage and Wagon Department. They maintain and repair carriages and wagons

DOME – District Outside Maintenance Engineers Department. They looked after all machinery used by the railway i.e. lighting, heating, machinery, cranes etc.

Duplex gauge – a gauge that showed two readings at the same time.

Fishplates – plates that are used to join two lengths of rail together.

Headshunt – a length of track used to access sidings without going onto a running line.

Hornstay – a stay across the bottom of the slots axleboxes moved up and down in to maintain the strength of the main frame and stop the axleboxes dropping out.

MFD – A hydraulic jacking system designed specifically for dealing with derailments and manufactured by Maschinenfabrik Deutschland. (See photos of Bedale derailment).

Multiple – When two or more locos are coupled together electrically so one driver can control them all from the leading cab.

Pul- Lift - a hand operated hoisting mechanism that could be used in many ways to lift or pull things. Available in various capacities 2 ton up to 10 ton.

P'way – The department that maintained the track 'Permanent Way' and surrounding land.

Roundhouse – Known as the Bullring (for obvious reasons) this was an octagonal building which housed a 70 foot diameter turntable leading to 25 stabling roads. Older designs were round and the one at Thornaby was the last to be built in Britain.

Sands – The driver could press a button and sand could be blown by air between the wheel and the rail to improve adhesion if raining or bad weather.

Secondman – Once steam locos disappeared the fireman was then called a secondman and assisted the driver (but actually did nothing). Eventually only certain turns had a secondman where his help was needed i.e. the tool vans.

Shedmaster – The manager totally in charge of the depot and its staff, drivers and all maintenance staff. In the mid 1970s it was re titled Depot Engineer who purely looked after the depot and maintenance staff, The drivers being put under an Area Manager along with the yard staff and guards.

Shunter – Double meaning for this a) a loco used for shunting wagons b) a member of staff that would direct shunting moves and couple and uncouple wagons.

Side Rod – Rods that coupled wheels together so that all the wheels rotated together.

Slides – Also known as beams. These were moved out of the crane chassis to increase the area of the crane base thus increasing its stability when lifting heavy loads. On steam cranes they were manually moved and also manually screwed down tightly onto packing thus ensuring the crane was stable.

Staithes – A North Eastern method of unloading house coal in goods yards where the wagons are above cells into which the coal could be dropped.

Swashplate - a type of hydraulic pump or motor that used a tilted plate to drive several small pumps at once.

Tool Vans – another name breakdown train. Usually composed of the following: - a riding van for the staff, a packing van to carry wooden packing, slings chains and all the other equipment to deal with derailments, a jacking van designed specifically to carry the MFD jacks and finally a crane. It would also refer to the road vehicles i.e. a 'Bruff' and or lorry. Different areas had different names for their tool vans...

Trackwork – the sleepers and rails fasten to them.

Warricks – An adjustable chain that could be attached under and to both rails to pull and hold them in gauge (i.e. 4' 8 ½") so that vehicles could be moved across damaged track.

Wheel drops – a method of lowering wheelsets out of a vehicle and via a system of tunnels getting them under a crane to be hoisted up for renewal or repair and then replacing them.

Wheelset – an assembly comprised of an axle and two wheels. On diesels a traction motor would be fastened to a wheelset.

Wheelskate – a small wheeled trolley that could be placed under a seized wheelset, holding the wheelset clear of the rail allowing the loco or wagon to be moved at 35mph to a depot.

Wrong Line – running in the opposite direction to the normal.

Diesel locos were originally described by the builders name and a classification type 1 to 5. In 1974 when a computerised system (TOPS) of managing trains was brought in all locos were designated by a class based on the original type.

Drewry 204hp shunter – later called class 03 or 04 depending on builder.

350hp Shunter – later called class 08 (BR built but with various engines fitted).

English Electric Type 1 – later called class 20

Sulzer Type 2 – later called class 25

English Electric Type 3 – later called class 37

English Electric Type 4 – later called class 40

Sulzer Type 4 – later called class 47

TAKING THE WEIGHT